110 NUGGETS for EXCELLENT PARENTING

With 120 Powerful Godly Affirmations and 160 Prophetic Prayers for you and your Children

Georginia Nwoke

Copyright © 2016 by Georginia Nwoke
Visit author's website at www.nuggetseries.com
Email: georginia@nuggetseries.com

110 Nuggets For Excellent Parenting
With 120 Powerful Godly Affirmations and 160 Prophetic Prayers
for you and your Children
by Georginia Nwoke

Printed in the United States of America.

ISBN 9781498463317

All rights reserved solely by the author. The author guarantees all contents are original and do not infringe upon the legal rights of any other person or work. No part of this Book may be reproduced or transmitted in whole or part in any form or any means, electronic or mechanical, including printing, copying, recording, or by any information storage and retrieval system without permission in writing from the author. The views expressed in this book are not necessarily those of the publisher.

Scripture quotations taken from the King James Version (KJV)
– *public domain*

www.xulonpress.com

This book is dedicated to our two sets of twins
1. Onyekachi and Onyinyechi,
2. Chinenye and Chinonye,
who God has used to teach me to be a parent and
I am still learning!

CONTENTS

ACKNOWLEDGEMENTS	ix
INTRODUCTION	xiii
EMOTIONAL:	23
BEHAVIOR	47
RELATIONSHIPS:	72
DIVORCED /SEPARATED PARENTS:	88
SINGLE PARENTS:	97
PARENTS IN ADDICTIONS:	101
PHYSICAL:	105
UNDERSTANDING DIVERSITY OF CULTURE:	113
TEACHERS AND PROFESSIONALS WORKING WITH CHILDREN FROM DIVERSE POPULATION:	116

110 Nuggets For Excellent Parenting

PARENTING CHILDREN WITH

DISABILITY: 121

VISIONS AND GOALS: 124

SELF ESTEEM: 128

FATHERS: 134

SPIRITUAL: 140

ALL PARENTS: CARING FOR YOURSELF

AS A PARENT 146

APPENDIX 1: POWERFUL GODLY

AFFIRMATIONS FOR YOU AND YOUR

CHILDREN 161

APPENDIX 2: THANKSGIVING PRAYERS AND

PROPHETIC PRAYERS FOR YOU AND

YOUR CHILDREN 171

ACKNOWLEDGEMENTS

The contents of this book had been in my mind for over ten years before I confirmed to myself that it would be helpful. My children, and a lot of people I have met in my career, have inspired me to put these thoughts down.

I want to thank my children, who have taught me through being honest with me, that parenting is experienced "on the job." I am grateful for the opportunity to learn through each of you at various times and, in some moments, from all of you at the same time. I specially appreciate my husband, Alfred, who God has used to keep me focused on His Throne of Grace!

I also want to appreciate every parent, child, teenager, and young adult across the globe, who have, at one time or another, given me the opportunity to learn from them.

I also want to thank my professional colleagues, my clinical supervisors, and the principals I have worked with in schools, colleges, and clinical settings in the last thirty years. It was very insightful to sit in those meetings with parents and their children, while at the same time watching and listening to the children unburden their minds and speak from the depths of their souls. Those moments are irreplaceable!

This book would not have been started at all, let alone published, without these words from my children: "Mommy, you have to put these things down in writing, it will benefit families and support other parents." Onyekachi, Onyinyechi, Chinenye, and Chinonye, who call me their "pia": I love you all dearly, you all are very special in my heart and will always continue to be.

Thanks to my friends, Peter and Shay Olorundimu, for those times you listened to me, gave me insightful feedback, and encouraged me to "just write." A special thanks to Chioma Uchendu and Chinenye Nwoke for doing the final editing of the manuscript. Thanks to my friends and professional colleagues across the globe, especially all of you who have supported us in our parenting role. I thank you for always checking on us! A special thanks to my special cousin, Ibis, and her husband, Chukwuma, for being there for us—we love you dearly!

A big thank you to my Pastors, Tubosun Sowunmi and Monisola Sowunmi, for the platforms and opportunities you have given me to work with you. Every assignment you gave me took me one step closer to writing this book for my fellow parents. I am most grateful! My gratitude also goes to my parents, Elder Erastus and Ezinne Keziah Osuala, through whom I started having some insight on how to be a parent. I appreciate my brothers and their families: Harrison and Julie Pepple, Rev. Dr. Theodore and Uloma

Osuala, Michael and Chika Osuala, Samuel Osuala, and my special Aunt, Mrs. Patience Cookey, who have always prayed that the Grace of God be multiplied in my life and in my family. I love you all for all your supports.

Finally, and most importantly, I am thankful to Almighty God for His Exceeding Grace and Love upon us. I am forever grateful to you my Father.

INTRODUCTION
TOUGH JOB, GREATEST GIFT

Parenting is the greatest role we start automatically to play, once our pregnancy test results are positive. As we feel the excitement of looking forward to holding our new and precious babies in our arms, simultaneously, our hearts are filled with multiple questions of how we can be those perfect parents that God has ordained that we become. Parenting is a role that we don't step into because we have enough experience. It is a role that we learn on the job, no matter what we have seen our parents do or how long we have supported our parents in raising our younger siblings. Couples, from the point they know they would be having a baby soon, begin to read books, ask questions, and go the extra mile to prepare for this new role. The question is how much preparation is enough?

As a little girl, I overheard my grandfather say that if not for the joy between a parent and a child, no one would raise another human being because it is such an overwhelming task. Each time I remember this comment, I tend to agree with what he said, being a parent myself.

Parenting is a continuous role. It starts with a baby; however, the task never ends, even when those babies evolve into adults with their own families. Even at that stage, you still worry about your children and their families, because they are always mom and dad's little girls and boys. In raising our two sets of twins, I have always worried, asking myself: are my babies going to be healthy as I give birth? Are they going to grow up healthy? What food are my babies going to like or enjoy eating? What school or daycare will my babies attend? Who will be my children's friends? What high school will they attend? What college? What career? Who are they going to date? Which city will my babies live in? When are my babies going to leave home? Who will they marry? Honestly, the number of questions that went through our minds was unending; right from the point the pregnancy test came out to be positive.

This book is written out of deep thought and compassion for families who are still challenged daily with so many questions about raising their children. How does a single parent play both roles as a parent if the other parent is absent, deceased or alive and refuses to get involved? The tips shared in this book are from the experience of being a parent, with my husband, to our two sets of twins that we had eighteen months apart! That was quick, wasn't it? We had four babies in our hands at the same time, basically. The first set is a boy and a girl, and the second set is two girls. They crawled and walked at different times. They are not identical in any way; they have different passions, gifts, and talents. We started taking all of them to doctors if one got sick with cold or flu; because we knew it would eventually go round. It was very challenging to breast feed; if I fed the boy first; there will not be enough breast milk left for the sister. I decided to allocate one breast to the boy and one breast to the girl and this allocation formula was also used for the second set of twins. Once any of them finished with their own side of the breast, and was still hungry, we supplemented with baby milk. That was a journey, and you don't want to imagine what I looked like, coupled with the sleepless nights.

I have always asked myself, if children are blessings from God, how come it is so taxing and challenging most times to think of what I need to do or say as a parent? There have been a lot of times that I needed my parents or someone else to parent me, and here I am standing on that pedestal of parenting my children. I don't know if anyone else has ever felt this way before, but I go through this most times. I have come to the conclusion that if God says that, "children are blessings that are given to us," there must be a special Grace from God as well that will always help us to meet this awesome responsibility.

My heart goes to families that are asking themselves: what did we do wrong? How can we get it right? My heart goes to those young couples who still have sleepless nights, and still have to be at work on time; and most passionately to those families with multiple births, with children who cry one after the other in quick successions. I feel the palpitating hearts of those parents who saw and received negative messages from their parents on how not to be a parent; and now they have vowed to get it right by making that conscious decision to swing to the positive side of the pendulum. These parents are working extra hard because they cannot offer what they don't have. How does a man who never had his father in his life learn to be a dad? How does a woman who never had a relationship with her mother learn to be a mother? How does a child raised by a parent who thinks he or she knows it all learn to be a parent himself or herself?

There is a way out definitely, and that is the focus of this book.

Most of the strategies shared in this book come from personal experiences, working with parents and children across the globe. My hope is that going through this book will give you the insight you have always thirsted for and your job will eventually be easier. You will be able to raise children who will be a joy to you, pass on the baton to your generations unborn, and a legacy will be left in your generational line even after you have gone.

My recommendation is that as you go through these nuggets, you will pause after each one to reflect on what you are doing currently, and think of ways you can apply these skills in line with your environment, because change starts with you.

Your children are little flower buds; they need your support to blossom into full flower petals that are attractive, with a pleasant aroma, full of purpose and the potential to reach the greatest heights they are created to reach. They need you daily as parents, grandparents, uncles, aunties, pastors, teachers, and professionals to get to that height.

This book has been categorized into areas of focus and responsibilities: Emotional, Behavior, Communication, Relationships, Divorced /separated, Single, Self Esteem, Fathers, Understanding Diversity and Culture, Physical, Visions and Goals, Spiritual, Caring for yourself as a Parent, Affirmations, Prayers and Prophetic Declarations with Biblical References from King James Version (KJV). My hope is that as you read through, you will reflect on each nugget and connect the dots in your own life, take daily steps to be that parent that will nurture the buds you have in your hands to blossom into full blown colorful petals.

NUGGETS

There is need for you and your spouse to understand that as your baby arrives, the dynamics of your relationship is very likely to change. This is because; there is now another human being that comes into your relationship, who will need your care and time. This is not the time to be in a pity party mode, or hold it against your spouse for not paying much attention to you anymore like what your relationship used to be. This is a time for joint effort and team work. This can be achieved by having a deep conversation about this anticipated change and your expectation from each other before the baby arrives.

Most couples expect so much from each other without having a prior conversation about each other's needs. This may bring a lot of tensions and disappointments in relationships while caring for the new born. For example, if as a new father, you have not asked your spouse to give you some time to rest after you get back from work before taking over the care of your baby, your spouse may feel frustrated that you do not jump in immediately to help out. Asking for what you need from each other will go a long way to understanding and caring for yourselves as you raise your baby.

Nuggets are personal experiences, suggested thoughts and clinical insights that have been put together to support you as you journey through parenthood. These insights can be applied as you parent your children, teenagers and even in your relationships with your young adults. Nuggets are practical, helpful and will support you in building strong lasting relationships with your children as they grow. Parenting is not just a physical journey; it is also a spiritual exercise which can only be achieved with wisdom from God. Nuggets incorporate affirmations or positive statements based on Biblical promises of God and prophetic prayers that will help you pray your children into their destinies. See Appendices I and II. As a parent, you have spiritual authority over the lives of your children. Nuggets will be explored from different aspects, starting with developing the emotional self of your children.

EMOTIONAL:

Our emotional self forms part of the core of our being. It is that part of us that can be happy, sad, scared, hurt, or whatever feelings we have, from to time to time. I call this the "little girl" or "little boy" inside each of us. It is your responsibility to ensure the emotional wellbeing of your children as they grow. This can be achieved through the following suggested steps:

1. Make your children feel emotionally safe. Your children need to know and be reassured that they are loved and accepted for who they are. Acceptance is recognizing your children for who

they are. Don't live your lives through your children. When your children hear you say, "you are my world", "I cannot live without you". This may put your children under a lot of pressure. Some parents want their children to go into the careers that they couldn't achieve as a parent. For example, some parents want their children to go to medical school, which they as parents couldn't achieve when they were the same age as their children. As your children grow, they will understand the feelings you have for them and it will be excellent for them to know that they are loved and accepted for who they are and not because of their achievements.

For example, as our children were growing up, we engaged the services of private lesson teachers to support them with sciences and mathematics because I struggled with physics in my High School. My plan was to give them that motivation to study medicine, engineering, nursing or any profession in the sciences, which I could not do myself, even though I wished for it at that time!

One of my girls went into Nursing and came back one day to say, "I don't want to do shift work; I am not cut out for nursing." The same year, our son called me while he was on public transit, coming back from his classes to say, "Mom, I want to change my course. I have found my passion in Sociology." I said, 'Son, it's your life. It doesn't make me love you less, just do what you love.' After I hung up, I thought, 'Oh my God! What a jump from Biological Sciences to Social Sciences.' I realized I had been vicariously living my dreams through my children. I took a deep breath and asked myself, 'Georginia, what have you been doing? Back off, it's not your life!' Afterwards, I resolved to hands off my children's career and provide support as they discover their individual career pathways.

As parents, we are only a guide or compass to our children. Instead of superimposing our choices or assuming roles as key decision makers, we should hold conversations that encourage critical thinking and enhance decision making skills. We can ask thought provoking questions such as: In what sectors of the economy can you work when you graduate? What is the income range for people already in that field? How valuable is your career choice to the society? It is their responsibility now to figure things out. If they don't like what they studied, they can always go back to school; it is their decision and I have backed off. Since then I feel no stress at all about their future careers, though the lessons helped to build their confidence in mathematics and sciences!

Are you doing the same thing like me? Give your children tools to discover their passion, equip them with skills for decision making and trust their decisions. This will make them connect more with you. I remember my son saying, "Mom, why do most parents want to choose what their children will study? You need to share your experiences with parents, so they can learn from your mistakes."

110 Nuggets For Excellent Parenting

2. As parents, don't ever call your children names; this may put labels or stigma on them and their lives. For example, if you tell your child that she is eating too much and she in fact, looks fat; or too little and looks skinny; the message your child will get from you is that she is fat and ugly. This child may start having feelings of low self-esteem, feeling ugly, start dieting, counting calories and battling with eating disorder for the rest of his or her life. This brings sadness to the child and your child will continue to hear your voice in his or her head for the rest of his or her life and may begin to eat comfort food to take his or her mind off the pain of your name calling.

One of our children when they were little, use to eat very little meals. We made sure no one in the family called her names; we continued discussing the importance of food in having good health, not just with her, but as a family. She eventually turned around at some point and started eating.

3. Your parenting style has a lot of impact on your children. When you are like what I call an "Iroko Tree Parent" over your children, you are too tough, too strong, unmovable and insensitive to the feelings of your children. They do everything to see the rays of light but your strong personality does not allow them to know who they are just as an Iroko tree does not allow other plants underneath it to see or experience the rays of sunshine.

Your child wants to know your reasons for saying 'NO!' Explain to them, they have the right to your explanations. For example, my own parents were, at a point in our lives, "Iroko Tree Parents." I still remember how my siblings and I felt. For us, we chose to give our children the opportunity to attempt to resolve their ambivalence, exploring the pros and cons of every behavior, in order for us to make an informed decision. This became a great step of building blocks in our relationships.

4. When you are an 'Iroko Tree Parent,' your children will be very afraid of you and they may begin to lose their sense of self-worth from very early age. This may affect who they become as adults. Your children's self-esteem may be negatively affected; which can be evidenced in passive communication styles and some un-resolved anger. I was initially an "Iroko Tree Parent"; trust me, it never worked; and my children shut me out of their world. I had to change my strategy to being more flexible and hearing them. From this point, they began to open up and we talk about everything. When we become so strong that our children cannot get through to us, they will resort to talking to their peers or their peers' parents. You can imagine what the outcome or impact will be on your child if these people your child is talking to, have negative core values about life expectations. This is how good children may end up having criminal records because it started from

finding themselves in the hands of unapproachable parents.

5. Barbara Coloroso (2010) in her parenting work on *Kids Are Worth It,* identified that there are also parents who are emotionally distant and not engaged in their children's lives. These types of parents believe that once they can provide for their children, it should be enough for them. Parents here are not emotionally involved in day to day raising of their children. Children raised by uninvolved or passive parents may be clingy and needy, have low self-esteem and may be rude due to unexpressed anger held against uninvolved parents. They may also feel less competent than their peers.

As a parent, the more you stay away from your children, the message you are giving them is that they are not as important to you as your jobs, businesses, careers, and investments. I was in banking for over ten years, and when we got to England from Nigeria,

110 Nuggets For Excellent Parenting

I shut the door to my banking career. I decided to go back to Education which was my first career so I could support them with school work and be home around the same time with them. This gave me opportunity to support them emotionally too.

6. Please do not compare your children with themselves or another child outside your home. Every child you have is a gift and each has a peculiar talent. Comparing your children brings division, breeds animosity and low self-esteem, in the life of the one that feels less than "the perfect child." In course of raising our two sets of twins, I almost fell into that trap of treating some better than others. I made up my mind that I will never do that because each of them is a special gift with special talents. From time to time, they will always ask me who I love most and I will always make them understand that I love them specially and equally too, even with their individual differences. Comparing your children breeds unhealthy

competition, jealousy, anger and resentment all through their lives.

7. According to Stephanie Covington (2008), in her work on addictions, children take on roles in a dysfunctional family as a way of surviving the pain they are going through. These roles are: hero, mascot, scapegoat and lost child. Do not create a hero out of any of your children. In most families, there is tendency to put the first child or one of your children on a pedestal of being a role model, caretaker for his or her siblings.

This robs your first child or whichever child the opportunity to be a child, growing up and looking after himself or herself. Your child hearing comments like, "don't you know that you're the first child; you are supposed to show a good example." The message this child is getting from you is that, he or she is supposed to be perfect and take responsibility for the mistakes or failures of your other children, or be a parent to your other children and sometimes "parent" you the parent. This is a huge task and can be very overwhelming to start at a very early age to be a care-taker to fellow children and even to you the parent. This particular child loses his or her sense of self or identity and finds self only in taking care of others anywhere she or he goes.

Understand that caretaking is different from caring for others. This is common in most families where parents are addicted to work or do multiple jobs, work long hours to make ends meet or to make money for investments, at the expense of raising their children and playing their roles as parents etc. This can also happen in families where the parents are in any form of addiction, such as alcoholism, drugs, or any form of abuse. Take a minute and reflect on your own childhood; what role did you play in your own family and how did you feel playing that role?

I am the first child and the only girl in my family. There were great expectations for me to look after my brothers. This caretaking behavior in me plays up all the time and only recently, did I become self-aware to recognize the brunt of assuming responsibility for other people's behaviors and mistakes. Now, I remind myself, that I am not responsible for other people's behaviors and mistakes; I am only responsible for me! In raising our children, each of them have their chores and they are held personally accountable. My son does the dishes as well as his sisters. There is no gander discrimination in assignment of chores and the expectations are very clear.

8. According to Stephanie Covington (2008), other roles that children can get into in a dysfunctional family are: the Mascot, who covers everything with humor, the Scapegoat, who has fun and behaves irresponsibly, and the Lost child, who enjoys being alone and withdrawn.

In my family, one of our children appears to spend time alone. Do not get me wrong, this child is a great kid! However, most of our time was spent worrying about this child that we failed to introspectively focus on the issues in our relationship as parents. I later realized that this child may be actually acting out what was going on in our relationship as parents, rather than our false perception of our child appearing withdrawn. This is actually what Stephanie Covington (2008), had identified as children who take on the role of lost child to be able to deal with dysfunctions in families.

I realized I had to start doing some work on myself, and I got a therapist who supports me from time to time to process my emotions in line with my own "little girl issues." Along the line, I realized I have my own trauma which I continue to work on. Things are better now in our relationship with this child; I wish I had started working on myself earlier! As parents there is need for you to understand that in every family, there is an element of dysfunction, it is just a matter of degree!

9. Understand that children raised by parents who were not available emotionally, may feel

110 Nuggets For Excellent Parenting

abandoned by their parents. Get me right; you may say "but I am always at home with them"! If you are emotionally unavailable, your children will feel emotionally abandoned. According to Claudia Black (2001), in her work on impacts of addictions in the family; children who grow up feeling emotionally abandoned have issues in future relationships.

These issues include fears of abandonments in their adult relationships, difficulty trusting because of broken promises from dad and mom growing up. Such children raised with abandonment issues also play victims in their relationships and they struggle with taking accountability for their actions. They always seek validation from outside of self because they never got it from dad and mom. They may also feel undeserving of love and care in their adult lives. It is therefore necessary that as a parent you are not just physically present but also emotionally available.

10. Emotional availabilty for your children can be achieved taking by interest in their world and being supportive during their challenges. There are times you just need to listen and allow them talk through their feelings and challenges. Be there for them. Don't steal their air time when they start talking to you. Don't talk about your own problems; allow them that time to talk through their problems and what they need to feel better.

Talking about your own problems takes the focus away from your child and your child feels unimportant. It is your child's time, respect it, and honor this time, please. Reaffirm their sense of self-worth by complimenting them where they have done well and getting them to reflect on steps they can take next time if the same situation reoccurs. Through this process you are being supportive and teaching them critical thinking at the same time. This strategy works really well in my relationship with our children.

11. Children see their parents as the first adults they have to trust. When they trust, they trust wholly and without limits. Some parents make it a routine to report their children to adults within other systems the child comes in contact with and these authorities confront their children directly. Examples include: the school teacher, the pastor, grandparents etc.

As a parent, most times this is your way of expressing concerns for inappropriate behavior your child is showing at home and asking for support. For the children, they see this as punitive, and a way of embarrassing and exposing them for their mistakes. At this point, you may lose their trust in you for being emotionally vulnerable. They may shut down on you, because they feel you enjoy breaking their confidentiality. Your children want to believe and know that they can always count on your trust.

Children who experience this growing up may begin to defy authority figures even as adults because they cannot trust any authority not to betray them.

As a parent, don't get me wrong; it is acceptable to seek support in raising your children. It is wiser to get the support and apply the insights yourself in raising your children. I always reached out to get supports, more insights and applied these insights myself. This helped me to continue to win our children's trust.

It is your responsibility and not anyone else's. You can get support through applying the nuggets suggested in this book, attending parenting courses, reading books, talking to professionals, other parents, and your pastors; apply the knowledge in your day to day interaction with your child and above all; ask God for wisdom, be a role model and pray for your children.

12. As a parent, can your children trust you for independence? Give them opportunity to try their wings like the eagle does to the baby eagle. How

110 Nuggets For Excellent Parenting

will your children learn to make decisions if they do not try making one? It is worse not to make any decision than to make one and fail. Help them to explore the lessons learnt in the decision that has failed, not criticism of the failure.

Remember, lessons learnt from the "wrong decision" will help them in future. If they fail, please make them to understand that life is a learning curve and there are more opportunities to try again. Critical thinking skills will help them like a baby eagle to try their wings. Starting early to encourage your children to make little decisions will help them to grow up to be independent adults who will always weigh consequences of their choices and decisions before executing each choice or decisions. This is another opportunity to grow and strengthen their decision making skills.

13. Let your children know when they make you proud. I am always open to identify progress in

whatever our children do, no matter how small it is. I text them, phone to verbalize my compliments even before they get home. I also use open ended questions to support them to identify areas for improvements. Sometimes as parents we struggle to say or give compliments to our children because, we did not get it from any of our parents growing up. We tend to practice what we have learnt and messages we received growing up.

When your children are successful and excited, share in their joy and show excitement too. It is not the time to remind them of an unaccomplished task or chore. It is not a time to remind them they had failed once. It is a time to rejoice and laugh with them. I have always been very excited for our children in their milestones of success, and encouraged them even when they think they have not done enough. The danger in not acknowledging the little progress your children make is that some of them will stop trying and shut down.

110 Nuggets For Excellent Parenting

14. Let's be aware that material gifts cannot take the place of emotional support for your children. As they grow they will get to a stage where they will realize that there is still emptiness at the core of their being and they will begin to look for someone to fill that hole. Usually at this stage, it is not a good story because whatever is available looks good and suitable for them. You don't want to imagine your children needing to fill this void when you will not be permitted to have a voice in their lives. At this point, anyone that says "I love you" seems to be a great candidate to meet the emptiness. This is why some ladies may go for men who have 10% of what they never got from their parents, thinking that this is the best they can get; with the notion that at least it is better than nothing.

15. As a parent, your words are powerful over the destiny of your child. A parent saying for example, "you are like your stupid dad. I wish I never had

you, you are a mistake" actually destroys the emotional self of your child. Your words can build or destroy your child forever.

When you speak negative words, your children are molded by your words and they eventually grow to become those words. This is because, when you speak negative words over your children, the angels of the devil will carry it and enforce it on your children. Parents when you speak positive words over your children, the Spirit of God will go ahead, take it and ensure that it is established in the lives of your children. Remember that your words are a reflection of your thoughts. Don't be surprised, children always remember the words their parents spoke to them, over them and they will always make that connection between the childhood messages they heard from you as their parents and what they turn out to become as adults.

16. Can your children talk to you when they are angry, feeling bad or upset with you? Are your children so scared of you that they cannot talk to you about their feelings? Are you raising your children to be seen and not heard? As parents we may be shocked that the greatest feedback we need for change in our lives can come from our children. Do you shut them down? Are we giving them the impression that they are rude because we don't want to hear the truth from them? Is your home an environment where children are taught "don't trust, don't feel and don't talk?"

According to Claudia Black (2001), in her work on addictions and families, these are the unspoken rules in a dysfunctional home. When a child experiences so much pain in the family, the child has to survive by stopping to feel. Also, there might be obvious issues such as abuse of all kinds going on in the family and the child is not allowed to talk about it. The family does not discuss or confront the abuser and the family

110 Nuggets For Excellent Parenting

life goes on, as if everything is "normal." In chaotic families, children stop trusting the adults in their lives because, promises are most times broken and the moods of these adults cannot be predicted.

17. Understanding your child's mood does not mean you should be sucked into his or her mood. Most times we scream and yell because our children are angry. When we do this we are not teaching the children emotional boundaries. We take on their emotions and at this point we cannot be supportive to meet their needs.

It is your responsibility to calmly ask your child when the child is in such moods, "What do you need right now? How can I support you?" When we do not have emotional boundaries as parents, we end up raising children who have no emotional boundaries. This means that when your children see you happy, because their dad is happy and sad because their dad is sad, they will grow up feeling sad when their

110 Nuggets For Excellent Parenting

friend is sad for whatever reason and happy when their friend is happy too.

This goes on into adult relationships, where you expect that you will be happy and your life will be complete once someone you have relationship with changes from inappropriate to appropriate behaviors. We all know that readiness for change must come from the individual and you have no control over people's behavior, you can only support them in meeting their needs and it is their responsibility to identify those needs.

BEHAVIOR

Every parent wants his or her children to behave appropriately as they grow. One thing to realize is that your child is naturally a good child. If your child behaves inappropriately, take your baby but throw away the behavior. Every mother in the delivery room picks up her baby and throws away the birth water. This will help you understand that things happening in the environment can affect your child's feelings and behavior. This will also give you some insights on how to support your child to change from inappropriate to desired appropriate behaviors.

18. When a child shows inappropriate behavior, as a parent, identify the need underneath the behavior being expressed by the child. This will give you more insight into steps to take in supporting the child's needs instead of reacting to the inappropriate behaviors.

For example, a child may suddenly start bullying peers at school. As a parent, there is need for you to look inwards. Has your child seen you argue or have a fight in your relationship? This may be a way your child is using to express his or her anger about the situation he or she is witnessing at home.

Look beyond the undesirable behavior and focus on goals underneath the undesirable or inappropriate behavior! Through this as a parent, you are able to redirect the child to meet his or her needs in a more appropriate way. There are some instances where you may notice that your child may be very angry at your pet or animal, slam doors each time the parents fight or have arguments in front of the child.

I recall a situation I regret deeply. My husband has been shuttling between our home and abroad in the last few years.

One evening I had a phone conversation with him which did not go well. As soon as our son got home, I started asking him why he did not notice that the garbage was full. All I can remember is that I immediately started to yell at him, and he left me there and ran upstairs to his room and slammed the door. I realized what I had done and said to myself, 'Georginia what have you done? You are losing your son! Really? Is he the cause of your aggression? Just be real with yourself!' I quietly went to my room, advised myself and gave him time to cool off.

The following morning, I went to his room and I said 'I felt disrespected when you walked out on me last night.' He said to me, "mom I didn't hear anything you said because you were yelling, raising your voice at me, that wasn't you! I am sorry if you felt disrespected, but that was the only way for me to deal with the situation." There and then I stepped up and took accountability for my behavior and I apologized to him.

How many times do we upset our children because of the negative emotions we carry and we have not taken steps to deal with our own emotions? It is your responsibility to ask for support for what you are going through and not dump it on your children. I have two therapists that support me from time to time and my Pastors are also a great support.

Your children need to talk about their negative feelings. If they are struggling to talk to you encourage them to talk to a professional who will be supportive to them in their challenges.

19. Be aware, that abuse has serious negative impacts on children as well as adults, and this is why the law takes it seriously. Your children may start displaying severe anger towards other children as a result of the pain, resentment and anger, which they have stuffed down, all through the time you quarrel and fight with your spouse. They

eventually become aggressive to peers, rude, and bully others, all in an attempt to hide their pain seeing you both being abusive to each other.

It is very common to see that aggressive parents end up raising aggressive children because this is the picture the children have seen growing up. According to Earnie Larsen (1991), in his work on impact of family dynamics on children's self-esteem, "children learn what they see, what they learn they practice, what they practice they become, and what they become has consequences."

20. Your body language as a parent also matters a lot when you speak to your spouse and children. Your children are watching the rolling of your eyes, the expressions on your face, the movements of our hands and they listen to the tone of our voice. All these make up the types of aggressive communications and negative messages they get from you as a parent.

110 Nuggets For Excellent Parenting

21. There is need for your family to establish common guidelines which is agreed within the family. Through this, common consequences are also agreed regarding the breaking of these guidelines. Children must be seen as partakers in establishment of these guidelines as a way of ensuring that their needs are recognized.

This will help to equip your children in developing skills for critical thinking, conflict resolution, establishment of boundaries and natural consequences that follow when these boundaries are crossed. Parents also need to be consistent in implementing the natural consequences as this will help the children to develop independence and be accountable for their actions.

22. A greater part of being independent is financial independence. Start early to make financial decisions concerning your children's future. Investing from their childhood makes their future bright. You can actually start to set money

110 Nuggets For Excellent Parenting

aside and invest for their future even before the babies are born. Start early to set money aside for Educational Fund, RRSP, Financial Literacy, and savings. Get them to account for their pocket money, learn early to invest and make profit. *Profit is better than wages!*

23. As a parent, make yourself accountable for your actions. I have seen instances where parents make mistakes and they blame the children for it and in fact, refuse to acknowledge that it is their fault. Children copy what they see and as a parent, you are the greatest role model. Children practice what they see and they eventually become what they have seen growing up. Do not make excuses such as you yelling because that is what you saw your parents do in your own family. You don't want your children going through the same things you went through. Be a positive role model, you are the God that your children see.

According to 1 Tim. 3:1–5,

"This is a true saying, if a man desires the office of a bishop, he desireth a good work. A bishop then must be blameless, the husband of one wife, vigilant, sober, of good behavior, given to hospitality, apt to teach, not given to wine, no striker, not greedy of filthy lucre; but patient, not a brawler, not covetous; one that ruleth well his own house, having his children in subjection with all gravity. For if a man know not how to rule his own house, how shall he take care of the church of God?"

24. As a parent, your children expect you to model accepting responsibility for your actions, e.g. apologizing when you make mistakes. Are you asking, 'apologize to my child?' Yes! I recommend exactly that. As a parent when you apologize to your child for your actions, you are showing your child opportunity to learn important skills for interpersonal relationships.

For example, you can accept responsibility by saying, 'I know I raised my voice at you this morning and I see that you are upset with me. Not brushing your teeth and having your bath on time makes all of us go late to school and work. I need us all to be quick in the mornings.'

This will encourage your child to take his own part of the responsibility and change the behavior of not being quick in the mornings. This has also given you an inroad into having that authority over your child. This way your child will trust and respect authorities because the child feels respected by you acknowledging your mistakes.

Some parents feel concerned that this may result in loss of authority over their children; your concern is right, but you will rather gain more authority over your child because you are building more trusting relationship between you and your child.

Do not get me wrong; you are not your child's best friend, but an authority that guides your child to navigate through life, modeling and teaching the child

110 Nuggets For Excellent Parenting

the skills he or she needs to discover self and fulfill destiny and purpose in life. You are a catalyst to that journey of self-discovery. As parents, let us not hinder our children's self-discovery.

25. As a parent, don't ignore positive behaviors, notice and identify them; reward and complement your child. Most times as parents we assume that our children know that we are proud of them and we don't have to say it, or they know we love them and we don't have to say it. Is it not ridiculous that we assume that our children have telescopes to see inside our hearts or are they mind readers?

As a parent, withholding complements for good behavior may lead to low self-esteem, and discouragement. This may create room for the child to turn to inappropriate behavior since the child now has the impression that positive or appropriate behavior does not attract your attention as a parent.

Many parents follow the pattern used by their own parents. You may say that your parents did not complement you and you still turned out well; I need you to reflect inwards. At that time, you were a child and was not complemented for appropriate behavior, how did you feel? Not complementing your children for appropriate behavior can make them to stop doing well in school and become delinquent. If you can't say it loud because you are not used to it and it is 'too heavy' in your mouth to say, write letters to them or buy cards and write words that express how good you feel about their behavior and progress. That will really connect you to their hearts and it helps them to know that you are proud of their behaviors or positive changes they are making every day, and that adults around them are noticing their hard work.

As a parent, it is your responsibility to change the negative patterns you experienced growing up; your surviving it does not make it acceptable. Change starts with you the parent and your children deserve better. You can break the cycle of negative patterns in your generation by doing something positively or appropriately different.

26. Give your children the opportunity to see you show good behaviors such as kindness to other people. Say nice things about people from all works of life, class and ethnicity e.g. talk about the good deeds someone you know did and let the children know how that made you feel. The world is a global village; you never know who will be there to meet your child's needs at a critical time when you are not close by. It is a small world!

If your children are able to show kindness, sympathy, give a helping hand too, e.g. share their toys; pray for a sick child in their class, pray for their school, their teacher, etc., let them know they made you happy and proud. Next time they will be willing to share, show kindness and repeat the same positive behavior.

Remember, gossip is negative and when we say negative things about people in front of our children, the message they get from you as a parent is that it is good to speak negatively about people. According to Sheila Hermes (2009), in her work on The *Art of Assertiveness,* gossip actually reduces self-esteem while assertive skills increase self-esteem. Choose what you want to see in your children.

As your children grow, teach them to give back to their community by volunteering in the homeless shelters, in churches, with the elderly, in your community etc. This will help your children to develop empathy, understand and appreciate the comfort that they have at home. Work with them to package gifts for other children in their community who are less privileged and also for the sick children in the hospitals. Through this, they will appreciate good health and live a life of gratitude.

27. Giving attention to negative behavior will always increase such behavior. Most children can use negative behaviors such whining, throwing

temper tantrums, crying, asking the same question over and over to get your attention. According to Barbara

Coloroso, in her work *Kids Are Worth It*, ignoring these behaviors can help your children learn appropriate ways of asking for their needs. Time out at the rate of the same minutes for the same age of your child can be used in addition to ignoring the child. Once a child is not supported by your attention when they behave inappropriately, the behavior may increase at first, because the child is still hoping for attention which is the usual pattern, but it will eventually stop.

Ignoring is effective for correcting negative behaviors if your child already has a close relationship with you. If not, your child will see it as a no-connection, which is the feeling the child usually gets from you as a parent. Combining ignoring negative behaviors with praises for positive behaviors will make ignoring an effective way for reducing negative behaviors. Once the child stops whining for example, praise the child for calming down and explain that when the child is whining, you cannot hear what the child needs and next time you will listen if the child can say what his or her needs are and you will support your child to meet such needs.

One of our children would cry and whine for any little thing. I recall ignoring this child each time and stoop down to her level, make eye contact and praise her when she stops her whining. Then I would say to her; 'when you whine, cry and throw tantrums, I cannot hear you and understand what you need. Next time if you can tell mom what you need, that will be awesome.' Then we will hug and I will attend to her needs.

All adults in your children's lives need to be on the same page on this strategy or else the child may get the attention of other adults who will come to rescue the child. In most families, grandparents are pulled into this cycle of tantrum by the child. For example, my parents who were very strict with rules are more relaxing now when it comes to my own children.

110 Nuggets For Excellent Parenting

28. No television or computer in your children's rooms. Do you wonder why? As they grow, you can't predict how many hours they will be up into the nights and this eventually may affect their whole energy level during the day. In as much as television provides opportunities for learning, positive role models, a bonding time for parents and children, it is recommended that the television and internet be in an area accessible to all family members and not in the child's room.

In today's world where computer games have become nannies for parents, children need to be redirected to understand that characters in the video games are not human and cannot provide the social and interpersonal relationship skills that they need to function as all round adults in our society of today. You may be raising the next CEO, Principal, President, Premier or Prime Minister!

110 Nuggets For Excellent Parenting

29. Discipline your child. Discipline is a set of instructions for the purpose of correcting a person and this person following these set of instructions is called a disciple. Always endeavor to be patient to show your children what they have done wrong and make them to be accountable or take ownership of their own part of the problem.

Involving the children in problem solving is very important. Through this, create opportunities for them to have options for solving the problem. Once this is done, the child will be able to see his or her mistakes and learn from that and will not repeat the same behavior next time.

Ensure that the child does not feel humiliated or embarrassed and this will help them to maintain their dignity. Correcting your children in the public will embarrass them, however if the child is unsafe, remove him or her from the situation. This confirms to us parents that our children also have feelings and they deserve respect too from us as much as we expect from them.

Finding time to sit with your child and talking to them to reflect on their behavior is more respectful and keeps their dignity intact. No human being likes embarrassment including your children. Sitting down and talking with our children was a great tool. Every discipline needs to be equivalent to the behavior. It must also be something that the child will learn from and correct the mistakes made. Don't kill a fly with a hammer!

30. Punishment makes the child feel that his or her parents identify the child with the bad behavior. Punishment creates the impression in the mind of children that parents have lots of power. When punishment is used, opportunities are not usually provided for the child to ask question and develop critical thinking, and as such doesn't develop skills for decision making. Usually in administering punishment, parents appear frustrated and angry.

When a parent hits a child who hits the sibling, the message that the child is getting is that it is acceptable to hit people and the parent's act of 'discipline' has confirmed that. This child grows up not learning healthy options for managing his or her frustrations, fears or anything that makes the child angry. These children may believe that their parents will have to make decisions for them including how to manage their feelings.

Children who are punished most times feel a lot of anger and resentments towards their parents rather than reflecting on the problems or the mistakes they have made and lessons they can learn for the future. Children who receive punishments from parents or adults around them may feel controlled and judged by these adults and they cannot wait to get out of this control! See every situation as a learning opportunity.

COMMUNICATION:

How you communicate with your children will affect their relationship with you as a parent. Communicating assertively with your children will be a way of showing them good example for learning effective communication skills.

31. Communicate assertively with your children using "I" statements. For example, say, "I need you to tidy your room," instead of saying, "can't you tidy your room?" This is another example of teaching them to communicate their feelings assertively.

According to Sheila Hermes (2009), in her work on *The Art of Assertiveness*, using the assertiveness formula "I feel . . . when you . . . because . . . I need

110 Nuggets For Excellent Parenting

. . ." will help your children learn to communicate appropriately. For example, if you say, 'I feel sad when you don't do your chore because it appears you have forgotten that we shared the chores. Next time I need you to take out the trash first thing in the morning or else I will cut down your TV time by one hour.' Through this, you are stating how you feel and you are asking for your need and the consequence that will follow. The child understands what you need to be done and the consequence is clear.

This strategy will help your child learn to communicate with other children and adults by saying for example "I feel sad when you use the computer at all times because I never get to finish my homework on time; next time I will appreciate it if you can take turns like the rest of us." Through this way the child learns to communicate his or her needs without being rude, focusing on self needs instead of using "you should" statements.

This will help your children to reduce the interpersonal conflicts in their relationships with other people, reduce stress, resentments, anger and bitterness because they can say "NO" without feeling guilty about it. People who communicate assertively have high self-esteem and no resentments because they are able to recognize their rights and communicate them without jeopardizing the rights of others.

You may discover that as you start communicating assertively with your children, they may cry or get angry. Whatever happens, remain assertive because their attempts are to get you to raise your voice or get angry etc. Assertiveness is not just a skill, it is an art and it works in all works of life, be it family, work, with your friends, name it! Children want to hear the correct thing they will need to do next time such situations come their way. When you scream, they only hear your anger and not the new ways of handling the situation next time.

32. Other communication styles that can affect your children negatively as identified by Sheila Hermes (2009) are passive aggressive, aggressive

and passive. Passive people avoid expressing their feelings and they end up pleasing everyone and people step on them always. They end up being resentful and angry.

Passive aggressive people are subtle and indirect; they always blame others instead of owning their own part of the situation. They can shut down and use silent treatment or appear to cooperate with you and are resentful. They never get to say how they feel and they can use sarcasm, instead of facing a problem and talking about it.

The aggressive communicator will always raise his or her voice, slam doors, being bossy, disrespectful, domineering and never considers other people's needs. The assertive communicator will always use "I statements" to communicate his or her needs, with a calm tone of voice, takes responsibility for his or own actions, stands up for self in a respectable manner. Your children will learn whatever

110 Nuggets For Excellent Parenting

communication style you model to them; you are the God they see.

33. As a parent giving constructive feedbacks will help your child to develop positive attitudes for behavior change. Don't be too critical. Criticisms swallow up your child's sense of self and identity. The child begins to see self as a failure and cannot please you the parent; your child may become demoralized, angry, resentful, and will start defying your authority or become emotionally detached from you and keep secrets.

These attitudes may become the safety mode for your child to always go to, in order to protect self. Acknowledging your child's emotions assures your child that you are still acceptable of him or her as a person. For example, saying something like 'I see that you are angry at John for ruining your toy, but it is not good for you to hit him; maybe calling John to play again with the other toy may make both of you happy.'

110 Nuggets For Excellent Parenting

Your children want to earn your approval; they want you to be proud of them. Just listening attentively and acknowledging their views and setting aside time on a daily basis to talk about things that upset them and things they found interesting or enjoyed will make them feel more accepted and open. They also expect you to talk about your day because this makes them feel and understand that you are human and can make mistakes too.

RELATIONSHIPS:

Relationship with God and fellow human is very important in our everyday lives. This is the connection we have with each other and with God. Relationship with your children is priceless and it can be a great support if it is positive or it can destroy them if it is negative, abusive and non-supportive.

34. Let your children know that you love them; don't be a miser with your hugs; your arms are created to hug. Hugs can heal; it is a way to say 'I love you' without saying a word. It can say I am always here for you, I understand your feelings, I hear you, and it can be a balm that soothes the

pain of life etc. So, hug your children and as they grow they will always ask for it and give you a hug too!

Once they have received it from you, even when they become parents they will continue to hug you and pass it on to their children too. It is a soothing balm. It breaks any barrier and this might be the purpose God had in mind for creating us with arms.

35. If you have multiple births like me such as twins, triplets or more, understand that your babies are all different individuals with specific talents and gifts. In multiple births, one may be an introvert and the other may be an extrovert. Do not ever compare them with one another like I said earlier. The temptations will always come to do this, but do not ever fall for it. They will upset you individually and as a group, but do not give in!

Always look for the positives in each child and highlight that to each of them. Through this you will be seen as open, transparent and unbiased parent. From time to time your children will trust you with their challenges individually; don't break their trust by gossiping about what they shared with you to their siblings. You end up losing their trust and belief in you as their parent.

36. At the end of the day when you get back home, process or talk with your children how their day went. This means talk to them and ask them how their day went. Use open ended questions such as "what" and "how," so they can talk without inhibition and not having opportunity to give "Yes" or "No" response.

I try as much as possible to avoid using "why" because it may make our children to feel that they have to defend themselves or like someone who is put in the dock in the court of law. When we use "how" and "what" questions, it helps the children and anyone actually to just talk and empty their minds.

Always provide opportunities for your children to have healthy conversations with you. This is a major source of memorable events that money cannot buy. Remember, giving your children gifts and money can NEVER replace your interactions with them as a parent and these gifts cannot fill the void you create when you make them feel that giving of gifts is what being a parent stands for. Buying a car for them when they turn sixteen cannot replace your day-to-day interactions with them.

37. Providing support to our children was a priority. At the peak of my banking career as I said earlier, going into education helped me to be aware of the curriculum our children followed in their schools, as a way for me to properly equip myself to support them. It worked out really well! You don't have to change your career like me; I identified my need and went for it.

This made them to be able to talk about their challenges with each coursework, assignments and projects; and we would always have conversations around each one and they felt supported.

According to Barbara Coloroso (2010), in her work *Kids Are Worth It*, there are three types of parents in a home. There is the supportive parent who will get into their children's world; connect with them and show concern for the children total well-being (physical, emotional and spiritual).

There is also the type of parent who is non-supportive and children have to figure things out on their own. The children from this type of home will prefer to speak to their friends, friends' parents than speaking to their own parents. In this type of home there is lack of emotional safety.

There is also the absentee parent! This type of parent may be under the same roof or home but is totally absent in the children's lives. Just for you to know, your children as they grow, they know if you are in their lives or not. They feel it to their bones.

110 Nuggets For Excellent Parenting

38. Help your children develop skills for friendships. Look for opportunities for you and your children to take part in community events like sports or summer camps, as this will help them build social skills outside school in a structured manner.

In choosing activities to engage your children, there is need to understand each child's personality to avoid them withdrawing from the activity as soon as they start. It has to be something they will enjoy or have passion for. A shy child may not be all out for these activities at first, but will rather enjoy activities that are more independent and involve less body contacts. This will motivate them to explore more activities and gradually get into more interactive games like football. Our son initially preferred playing at home, as he grew, we gradually introduced him to football and now this is one of his best games.

39. Showing your children how to interact with people can be a great tool for teaching them

social skills. For example, as a parent you can model shaking of hands, making eye contacts and demonstrating physical boundaries using arm's length with your child.

Model taking turns to speak and listen while focusing attention on the child as the child speaks. Ask questions that can help your children reflect or think back about a situation that happened to them. For example, 'it appears you felt frustrated with the way your friend handled the situation.' This will help to teach your child conversational skills and connecting to their feelings.

40. Find time to watch the programs your children enjoy with them. In these days of rat race, both parents need to make out time to watch their children's programs with them. This provides opportunities for you to explain using real life examples to teach the children about how to be kind to others.

Use 'how' and 'what' questions to invoke curiosity in your children regarding the behaviors of the characters in the program you are watching with them or in the book you are reading with them or to them. This is another way of teaching your children critical thinking and differentiating between appropriate and inappropriate behaviors. Identify characters that are showing good behaviors, emphasize on characters that communicate assertively.

41. As a caution, do not force your children to be friends with everyone in their class, church, or wherever they go. Just as everybody is not your friend, your children have the right to choose their own friends. Please respect this, in as much as you have the right as a parent to redirect your child if you notice that some friends may be a bad influence on your child. This brings us to family values.

42. As a family, what core values have you put in place or modeled to your children. At this point,

110 Nuggets For Excellent Parenting

ask yourself what your core values are. Children will usually take after the core values of their parents and what their family has as core values. Do the core values for your family include integrity, respect, care, trust, unbroken promises, hard work, kindness, spirituality, honesty about feelings? Children are heard not just seen? This list is inexhaustible (add yours).

The core values we inculcate in our children are what they bring to the table anywhere they go, including their adult relationships. When your child meets anyone, within five minutes the values you have taught them will show clearly. In every family some foundational core values will be helpful. These are: boundaries (parents and children having limits within which they can operate), sharing the Word of God, praying with them in the morning, praying with them at night, reading bed time stories, respect for one another, support for one another, etc. You can add

110 Nuggets For Excellent Parenting

to this list. It will amount to parenting suicide if you as a parent have no core values!

43. According to Claudia Black (2001), in her work on addictions and families, children who grow up in a family filled with promises broken all the time grow up not knowing how to trust in their relationships. Children who hear, "if you cry I give you something to cry about" become adults who shut down their feelings and turn it inwards because they heard as children that it is wrong to cry.

Children who hear 'NO' at all times without explanations or because mom says so, may shut down and will not bother to talk or ask questions even when they become adults. What type of children are you raising at the moment? It is acceptable for children to cry because that is the main way they can express their sadness, and they laugh and play when they are happy.

44. Give responsibilities to your children and hold them accountable. Let every child know what

their chore is within the family. Appreciate and say thank you once they have done it. If you need to remind them, assertively say for example 'John, I need you to do your chore and let mom know once you're done, ok!'

Asking questions such as 'why have you not done your chore' puts the child on the defense stand, feels judged and the child begins to come up with reasons why the chore is not done. This leads to apportioning blames; nagging and the child find ways of refuting the blames and then fight for a win with you. Your priority is to increase appropriate behavior and not to win a fight.

45. As a parent, do not be overprotective. Allow the child to play with other children. Are you one of those parents who will not allow their children to splash water on themselves in summer, play in the back yard for the fact that their children will get dirty? Is this about your own feelings of

what people will say about you for not being a great parent?

This may come from your own feelings of insecurity or low self-esteem or is it about your children's feelings? Ensure that your reason is right and don't make your children miss their memorable childhood moments. Don't get me wrong, it is your responsibility to protect your children and not compromise their safety. However, some parents are over bearing.

Children whose parents are overprotective may never practice or learn how to solve problems on their own, and these children get the messages that their parents can't trust them to make the right decisions. Every parent wants to raise a child who becomes an independent adult. When parents become overprotective, they struggle to let go of their children. In turn, the child's confidence may not increase because the child believes that she or he needs the parents for every little decision. Such parents always want to have inputs in everything the child does, career, job, even marriage.

As a parent, you can use open ended questions to get your child to see aspects where the child could be making a mistake and the child will get the insight and develop critical thinking pattern. For example, 'what do you like about your friend?' 'What do you like about your choice of career?' 'How much do people in that field earn?' 'Will you be able to run your own office if you study that?' These will awaken curiosity and critical thinking in your child for more information to make an informed decision.

For your teenagers, time will come when they will want to attend dinner parties; you must be seen as supportive while at the same time setting necessary healthy boundaries with them for safety purposes. Offer to drive them to the dinner venue and offer to pick them up after, at a specific time. If they don't see you as supportive or meeting them halfway, they will conspire against you, attend the party and switch off their phones if you try to call them and yell.

From my own experiences with our children, the battery in a teenager's phone is most times dead! There must be a conversation about safety for them and let them know you are concerned for their safety. This will make them to see it as their responsibility to let you know where they are at any time and they will let their friends know that, as our children will say, "It is getting late, I have to call my mom now so she won't worry." They see calling me as a way of helping me not to worry, but to me I see it as 'a safety check in.'

Children, who think in this manner, do so because there is already an existing intimate relationship between them and their parents. I used to dose off with my eyes half open, watching the time to go pick our children from birthday dinners or meet them half way at the train stations. They were always grateful. They were also at age when they could have made a decision to leave home, but they felt supported. This strategy worked greatly in raising our children.

110 Nuggets For Excellent Parenting

46. Children are valuable and always the only future human race has to offer. The greatest gifts you can give your children are the roots of responsibility and the wings of independence. In these days of social media, don't stop your teenagers from having Facebook account. All you need is to set necessary boundaries, agree on appropriate age and have conversations with them about your trust in them. It is also necessary that you be on Facebook yourself, as this will give you the opportunity to know their friends. As a parent you are there to be the compass and show your children the positive directions of life, so they can grow to make the right choices and decisions for themselves.

47. Patience is a great virtue. Teach your children to have patience. For example; wait in line with them when you are waiting to get your prescriptions from pharmacy, or waiting to see your Doctor. Do not always give them phone, IPad or

any electronics to play with. This can be a once in a while respite.

Understand that these do not encourage them to develop social skills, such as having a healthy conversation with people. In this world of instant coffee, instant tea, instant food, we are also building instant coping skills in children by keeping them silent with electronics.

Some children are growing up making more friends online than they have in real life. Imagine what will happen in the next three generations. They can only learn to have healthy conversations by practicing with family members and people outside the home, and there is need to create the opportunity for them to have real connections with people.

DIVORCED/SEPARATED PARENTS:

The amount of work required from divorced or separated couples is definitely much more, if children are involved. Both parents need to understand that your babies need to be nurtured despite the pain you both have within you.

48. If you are separated and your children spend some days in the week with each parent, both parents must have a common ground where they reach consistency to parent the children in terms of discipline, care and core values. Agree on guidelines that will be used in the two homes in order

110 Nuggets For Excellent Parenting

to ensure consistency. If not, your children will manipulate the situation knowing that you both either do not compare or check out information.

Discipline and consequences for breaking rules must be agreed and followed in both homes. Children know when you allow them get away with everything. Parents need to communicate for the purpose of raising children who are well behaved as part of the society and excellent leaders of tomorrow.

You may be divorced or separated, but you may also be raising the country's future president! You are both responsible for making those God given petals in your hands to blossom. This goal must override your feelings for each other and whatever may be the reasons that led to your separation.

49. Co-parenting is not easy especially after a bitter experience with your ex-spouse, but for the benefit of your children to continue to feel secure, loved and nurtured; co-parenting appears to be

the best. Never put your children in the middle and use them as weapons to get even with each other. As your children grow they will know the truth and will want to get away from both of you.

Speaking negatively of your ex-spouse to your children when they spend time with you may appear to work for you initially. As the children grow, they will always remember that you spoke negatively about their other parent and you will eventually lose out because they will always figure out the truth on their own.

50. Divorce or separation can be very painful. For your children's healthy development, never dump your pain on them by discussing your ex-spouse with them and what your ex-spouse did wrong in the relationship. It is always very easy to be sucked into this type of behavior, but it is unhealthy and can actually damage the children the more.

Get professional help where you can talk freely about your feelings, deal with it and heal. Remember healing does not mean that the pain never occurred; it means you have come to a point in your life where you no longer allow the pain and the effects from it to have power to control your daily lives.

When you go for help from a professional or from your mentor or your Pastor, ensure you listen and accept feedback in the area that you are accountable and ensure change starts from you and not your partner. Doing the same thing, the same way and expecting a change is actually being in a state of insanity. Professional help will also support you to identify the skills you need for the future and how you can work together effectively with your ex-spouse to raise your children.

51. Remember that whatever led to your separation also affected your children. Understand that their feelings matter a lot in who they become as adults. There is need for you both as parents to

110 Nuggets For Excellent Parenting

set up professional help for your children to talk about how they felt and how they can move on and have effective strategies for coping with the situation in the family where they once felt safe and secure.

The same way you are grieving a marriage or relationship that you lost, is also the same way they are grieving the loss of a home where they once felt safe and secure. If this is not done, your children may start acting out, bullying themselves at home and even in school; their grades and academic performance may be adversely affected.

In fact, all other negative behaviors including drugs and alcohol use can snowball from the separation and they can begin to have problems with the law. They may begin to expose their lives to risky relationships and even all kinds of abuse.

52. In parenting with your ex-spouse, be assertive in your communication style, in that way you don't

110 Nuggets For Excellent Parenting

feel resentful, get angry and shut down. Ask for what you need from each other and active listening from both of you is necessary for communicating effectively. Shared custody is recommended so long as the children are safe with each of you; there is no abuse (physical, mental, emotional, sexual, verbal etc.), alcohol, drugs, pornography involved in each parent's home. Remember, safety of the children is the utmost priority.

53. In your conversations, your focal point must be your children and in having such meetings and conversations, purpose not to get angry. Use all your grounding techniques to stay grounded and calm all through. This may not be easy but it becomes better as you continue to practice. Techniques like taking a deep breath, recalling God's promises for you, practicing gratitude, identifying what you see in your environment.

Above all pray and meditate before the meeting or phone call, asking God to help you. It is a tough journey to take once children are involved, but I know there is a Grace from God for every family going through this situation. Tap into this Grace on a daily basis by living a life of surrender to God and trusting in God's care, provisions and mercy.

54. In co-parenting, understanding and cooperation is very important. Don't punish your ex-spouse for every little thing. Also remember that keeping two homes can be financially daunting. Budgeting can be very useful, make it realistic and keep reviewing it.

Your children are growing daily; getting clothes from consignment stores, buying things for them during sales, toys from garage sales can be a great option. Don't be all out to punish your ex-spouse because he or she is paying for spousal and child support. It is very easy to fall into this trap and see this as an opportunity for revenge.

110 Nuggets For Excellent Parenting

55. Remember that your children are at the center of your fights. Learn to appreciate each other in the work of nurturing your children. It will be good to appreciate your ex-spouse for taking time to look after the children. The same way, it will be nice to say thank you when you get that child and spousal support from your ex-spouse. We appreciate people around us that we don't have anything that bind us together, how much more spouses that we have children with. This may be hard, but it is a great gesture to do. This will encourage your ex-spouse to continue to thrive in taking care of and providing for the children.

56. Your divorce or separation may have more negative effects on your children if you both argue and quarrel in front of your children, even over the phone. Children have a way of knowing who you are speaking to over the phone. There is need for you both to make your children understand

110 Nuggets For Excellent Parenting

that there is a plan from both of you as parents to continue to be in their lives.

57. Never threaten your children with anything that makes them feel unsafe. If your children feel safe with you and do not feel safe with their other parent, don't threaten to send them back to the unsafe parent. This will make them to lose trust and sense of safety in you who they feel safe with and trust. This will also make them to become scared, begin to look for safety and trust outside both of you.

SINGLE PARENTS:

There are lots of challenges faced by single parents; these may be from the loss of a partner or the partner has refused to be involved in the children's lives due to one reason or the other. Whatever situation you have found yourself as a single parent, there are some specifics that are worthy of note:

58. If you are doing multiple jobs to meet up with your finances; ensure the safety of your children as you shuttle from job to job. Ensure that your child care is trustworthy and safe. Sometimes, even when the children report how unsafe they feel, as parents we struggle with believing the

children. Every feeling of being unsafe must be taken seriously, if not your children can never trust you again.

59. Use your support network to help you with raising your children. Raising children is a community effort; let your church members, neighbors and your own parents support with respite care. At least once a week create time to do something for yourself, from going for coffee, to having a nap and doing some other forms of self-care.

60. Enroll your children in community development programs. Involve your children in volunteer programs with the homeless, sick children programs; these will help to develop empathy in your children and get them to appreciate your hard work and what you are able to provide for them.

61. Explore all the financial support and benefits you can get from the system. There are lots of Government programs and services, which

include financial benefits that provide supports in various areas to single parents. There are also some charities which provide various supports to women and men with low income for clothes, food, job search etc. Check your community center near you for more details. If you live in a country or locality where these supports are not available, be vulnerable and open to ask for all kinds of support from whatever community groups you go to such as your church, home groups, etc.

62. If you are seeing someone as a step towards starting a new relationship, gradually introduce this person to your children, when you are sure he or she is the right person for you and your children. If you are a single man, your daughter may feel your relationship with another female will take away your attention from her. This is the same for boys if their mother is starting a relationship with a male friend.

As a parent take it seriously if your children draw your attention to any kind of abuse, which may sometimes be sexual. Please do not dismiss them as childish talks; if you do, you will be damaging your children. Whichever way this affects you, ensure you don't lose the confidence of your children. If they do, they may become very angry with you, begin to act out, leave home earlier than you imagined.

They may get into the wrong crowd as a way of registering their non-acceptance of your new relationship. Do not get me wrong; there are also some situations where it works out for the entire family, especially if they are able to blend in and the children are in acceptance of their new step-parent; everyone is happy. Pray, hear God and take it gradual, and be sure of your decision in this area.

PARENTS IN ADDICTIONS:

Whatever you are addicted to takes away your attention from your loved ones. Addiction is an obsession of the mind with a particular behavior or substance. It robs your children the opportunity of having their parents present in their lives.

63. Addiction is continuously engaging in a behavior all the time or repeating the patterns of these behaviors despite the negative consequences of such behavior. A behavior can be an addiction if you are doing something that you do not have the courage to discuss openly with people around. You

may realize that the more you do it, the more you are drawn to it and you cannot stop it on your own.

Addiction can permanently take you away from raising your children and the addictive behavior takes away the attention you would have given to your children. Are you addicted to drugs, nicotine, pornography, alcohol, work, internet, social media, shopping, food, relationships, violence and abuse etc.?

You may be a functioning addict, for example you drink your alcohol or use your drug of choice after putting your children to bed, or watch your porn late in the night and still have intimacy with your partner. So long as your mind is obsessed with this behavior and it takes a lot of attention from you; you may be into addiction. It can even be your coffee and the fact that you cannot function without it.

If you are involved in any of these, be well informed that you are not available for raising your children. These are all ways of escaping from the real problems underneath your soul. Seek help and deal with it.

When a father stays out all day at work and comes back, have dinner and stays on Facebook, any other social media or continue work at home, your children will be longing for the presence of their father, who is physically present but absent in the children's lives.

Beware! In families where there is any form of addiction, most times, according to Stephanie Covington (2008), in her work on impacts of addictions on families, a child in that home steps into the role of the addictive parent. If the father is an alcoholic for example, most times the first child steps into the father's role to meet the mother's emotional needs, care for her and enforce discipline on the younger siblings. In doing this, the needs of this child are pushed aside.

In most dysfunctional families, this relationship with the non-addictive parent may lead to emotional intimacy, where the parent will begin to talk about his or her pain with this child and rely on this child for emotional support. If you are the non-addictive parent, please get professional support to deal with your emotional issues and don't dump it on your child. If you are addicted to anything, get the help you need by being honest with your challenges and getting the support you need to be free, so you can be emotionally and physically available to be an effective parent to your children.

PHYSICAL:

The physical self is another big aspect of your children's lives. 1 Corinthians 6:19–20, states that, your *"body is the temple of the Holy Ghost, and you have to Glorify God in your body."* In parenting your children, their bodies need to be nurtured as they grow. These can be achieved through the following:

64. Boundaries are limits within which your children can operate and feel safe. Set ground rules for your children, this will put structure in their lives and bring the awareness of consequences that follow. This will transcend to other relationships that they will have outside the home. Get them

110 Nuggets For Excellent Parenting

involved, get their inputs or suggestions. This will make them committed to being accountable for obeying these rules within the family.

There are times when you need to step up and be the parent. Your children will appreciate you for this as they grow. It is not beneficial for parents not to care about what their children are doing, especially when you are working all the time and sending them to babysitters. When children have the feelings that you do not care about what they do, they are likely to get into the wrong crowd.

65. There are parents who allow their children do whatever they like. These parents cannot say 'NO' to their children and they are easily manip- ulated by their children, always trying to please them. Barbara Coloroso (2010) in her work on parenting styles refers to this style of parenting as "Jelly fish." For example, if parents allow one child to do whatever he or she wants but they

enforce rules on the other child, the difference will show clearly as the children grow. Most times a child that is raised with some boundaries or limits is likely to achieve more than a child without boundaries. Enforcing boundaries selectively in your children can evoke jealousy between siblings.

66. There are also parents who are involved in their children's day to day lives. These parents set limits and boundaries and consequences are made clear. Parents negotiate with their children when necessary and children are given the opportunities to make choices and consequences of each choice are stated clearly to the child or teenager. For example, as small as asking your child, do you want to wear your red shirt or your green shirt? The two shirts belong to the child, so it does not really matter to you which ever shirt the child wears.

The power of choice prepares your child to start making decisions as they grow. This style of parenting gives the child the foundation to develop independent thinking and decision making skills. As your children grow, your parenting role will evolve to that of an advisor.

67. The children raised in families where parents are the main supports, feel empowered, have boundaries, are capable of making decisions as they grow. They have no problems with asking for support from their teachers and professionals who work with them. They can easily identify their needs and ask for resources and supports for meeting these needs.

As a parent, making clear what you expect from your children will help them to understand what you need from them. They will work towards nothing if you have no expectations from them. Barbara Coloroso (2010) identified six critical messages every

110 Nuggets For Excellent Parenting

child wants to hear: "I believe in you, I trust you; I know you can handle it, you are listened to, you are cared for and you are very important to me."

68. Children also expect you to live by example. Your children will learn from seeing what you do. If you have a curfew for your teenagers, specifying when they should be home; you cannot on your own part have late nights, unless you are at work which the children must also know. This is all about being accountable and responsible.

69. Another thing to consider in terms of physical boundaries is safety of your child at home. This can be achieved by child-proofing your home and environment. Have child locks on your door handles, child proof your electrical sockets etc. Understand that your babies will stick their fingers into these sockets because they are at the age of exploration and adventure.

110 Nuggets For Excellent Parenting

For us, it took a lot of work from us, our baby sitters and my mother to ensure our children's safety during this period. With four babies aged between 18 months and 1 month, it was a lot of work because they were all over the place as they grew daily.

70. As a parent, be very mindful of the body image you present before your children. Please, never stand in front of the mirror complaining about your weight, birth marks, etc. Your child hearing you do this, may make your little girl or boy to start dieting, in order not to be "fat" like mom or dad. Do some exercises with them that can help them to be happy or have insight about who they are.

For example, you and your children can identify and mention five or ten things they like about themselves. If they cannot remember anything, tell them that they are good helpers, that they have a sense of humor, or that they are good huggers etc. This will encourage your children to believe in who they are and feel beautiful in their own skin.

71. Have a family meal time. Eat fruits and vegetables in season. Children eat better when you eat with them and make the food colorful. Starting early to teach them to eat healthy and when they grow they will be used to this pattern of healthy nutrition.

72. Have a family time to exercise, play together, laugh, and walk the dog with the children. These are mostly activities that you do not need to buy with money. Apparently, children will always remember fun times together as a family than buying them a car when they graduate from high school as I said earlier.

Our son still recalls a time we went on weekend away to a beach, played all kinds of games as a family. He was about eight at that time, but he still recalls outrunning his father in football. It was fun. This memory for him is irreplaceable. If you don't start now to do things together with your children, by the time they leave home, they will rarely call you because they don't have anything to discuss with you. At that time, be aware that your career or business will not have a voice to speak back to you.

73. What is the atmosphere in your home? Create an environment where your children can laugh and play. According to John .F. Kennedy (1963), the late President of United States of America, had a silver beer mug with this inscription from the *Ramayana*: "There are three things which are real: God, human folly, and laughter. The first two are beyond our comprehension. So we must do what we can with the third." Laughter can bridge the gap between you and your children. Make your home a fun environment where everyone can be real, show their true feelings, and get the support they need without being judged by anyone.

UNDERSTANDING DIVERSITY OF CULTURE:

We live in a world filled with diverse population and immigration around the globe has increased our intercultural interactions. If your family has moved from your culture of origin to another culture, how do you support your children who are confronted with new cultural practices?

74. Understand that children and teenagers in Diaspora or in migration are facing the challenges of living their lives in-between two cultures; culture of their family's new home which may be Western most times and culture of their family of origin.

Take time to understand the culture of your new environment which your children face in school and in the mist of their friends as this will prepare you to understand what your children and teen-agers are exposed to on a daily basis.

As a parent, if you and your family migrated to a new environment, note that your children may adapt to the new culture faster and more easily e.g. change in their phonics, learn the new language faster than you the parent, their style of dressing may change, etc. This may create conflict between you and them.

Take time to understand the culture of your new environment so you can gain insight on how to relate with your children. This is necessary because enforcing your culture from your country of origin all the time will bring friction between you and your children. Create a balance and take the positives from both cultures and find ways of supporting your children because it is also a challenge for them adjusting to the new culture and environment.

I took time to learn the cultures of England and North America where we had migrated to as a family. These gave me more insights on how to support my children and set necessary boundaries.

Let the standard of God be your guideline for you and your children. Teach them the culture of God which transcends every nation and every culture; they will appreciate it as they grow. The culture of God is about having a Spiritual connection with God, having integrity, believing that God loves them no matter the country or culture or race they come from. It is about resting in God's Great Love.

Proverbs 22:6 says;
"Train up a child in the way he should go: and when he is old, he will not depart from it."

TEACHERS AND PROFESSIONALS WORKING WITH CHILDREN FROM DIVERSE POPULATION:

Our schools are becoming more diverse than we expect on a daily basis. This is also becoming more challenging for teachers and professionals working with your children. Teachers and professionals are trained currently to work with diverse population. In addition to their training, there is need for these professionals to understand a few more things.

75. Teachers and all professionals working with children need to understand that most families

110 Nuggets For Excellent Parenting

in Diaspora may have used a parenting style or a combination of parenting styles. This may have a few positive and negative impacts on the children you are teaching or working with. Some children you work with may be somewhere on the continuum, some may have parents who encourage the power of choice and critical thinking by the child on one end and another child may have parents that make decisions for the child on the other end. This will affect how they interact and the general dynamics in the classroom.

76. As teachers and professionals that work with children in Diaspora, understand the influence of cultures on their behaviors. For example, some cultures, do not allow a child to make eye contacts with adults when the child is being spoken to.

There is need to understand that lack of eye contact in some cultures is not a sign of learning disability. These children need to be supported to learn and understand that making eye contact is not disrespectful in the culture of the West where they live presently with their parents.

77. Teachers and professionals working with children in Diaspora need to understand that most families in Diaspora do not relocate at the same time. Most times the mother lives in the West or country of migration with the children. The father may still shuttle between what the families had known as home and their new home where they have migrated to. This arrangement may continue pending when the mother gets a good job before the father can relinquish his job to join the family.

This may actually take some years, even up to five years and in some cases the father may not join the family at all. He will continue to visit as often as possible until the children grow to adulthood, graduate from college and leave home. The children may see their father as that person that comes to solve

110 Nuggets For Excellent Parenting

problems and off he goes. They may not care to connect with their father emotionally, because he will be going back to where he came from anyway.

This structure usually gives mixed messages to the children because the father is not involved in the children's day to day lives. Thanks to Skype, FaceTime, etc. These technologies improvise to make up for lost times, but it cannot take the child on a ride to soccer games, piano lessons or to any other extra-curricular activities.

As professionals working with these children, there might be times when the child will have down time because he or she is missing the father. The child may also have down time if the child observes that their mother is not happy for some reasons with the current situation of the father working abroad and the mother raising him or her in their new country where the family has migrated to. These feelings that are external will affect the child's focus in the classroom and the child will need to be supported.

78. The entire family not being together as the children are growing can impact the emotional development of the children. The boys and the girls are growing without the emotional support from their fathers.

The implication of this is that the day to day emotional supports these children need from their fathers may not be present. This may manifest in forms of feelings of abandonment, rejection, lack of acceptance, difficulty trusting people especially males; not focusing in class, anger, low self-esteem and lack of interpersonal skills.

According to Claudia Black (2010), in her work on abandonments, the pattern is usually carried over into adult relationships and people involved become clingy, hyper vigilant, fear of loneliness and expecting to be abandoned in one way or the other at every step in their relationships. These children can also act out in school or at home as a way of expressing their feelings around their inner pain or fear and lack of emotional safety.

PARENTING CHILDREN WITH DISABILITY:

Are you parenting a child with disability? Have you been asking yourself and God a lot of questions? God is in that situation and understands your pain and stresses.

79. It can be very challenging to parent children with disabilities. It can be very hard most times to play this role with joy as you see your baby struggle through life. It is most challenging too if you are a single parent. Understand that you can only do your best.

110 Nuggets For Excellent Parenting

It is also very easy to always focus on this child at the negligent of your other children, which is not intentional but out of great compassion for this particular child. Being conscious of this divide, will help you start paying attention to your other children. Understand too that your other children can be overwhelmed and even angry as they help you in supporting their sibling with disability. It can be draining and overwhelming, not just for you, but for your other children as well. It makes them grow up too quick by stepping into adult roles.

80. This means that you and your other children will need respite and support from time to time. At least, once a week when you can, have someone help to watch over your child with disability. The respite can join you all for a time out and this respite will focus on your child with disability, while you take a breath of fresh air.

110 Nuggets For Excellent Parenting

As a parent you can also have a 'me' time when you connect with friends and family while the respite supports you with the children. Recharging your energy from time to time is very important in your role of parenting, and if you are parenting a child with disability, you need a double dose of physical and emotional energy.

81. Please do not see your child with disability as a punishment for your sins; Jesus Christ has paid the price for our sins. Get support in processing your feelings around this; talk to a professional, your Pastor e.tc. Understand that your child did not choose to have a disability, understand that he or she is special too before God.

VISIONS AND GOALS:

A parent without a goal is the same as a blind leading a blind. Our children expect us to show them how to dream and have expectations for the future. We are meant to instill hope in them and not despair. Get them to start with little goals such as getting up and making their beds, doing their chores, reading a book a month, learning to swim etc. Make it fun!

82. As a parent, have expectations for your children and encourage them to have expectations for themselves. Get them to make vision boards for themselves. For example, in the next six months,

one year, two years or more, where do you see yourself? Get them to start with short term goals. They can demonstrate these with pictures or write out where they see themselves in future. It might be pictures of high school, good jobs, happy family etc.

Let each of them share their visions and goals with the family and remember what each of them has said and lift it up in prayers during the family prayer time. Through this strategy, the children will always remember that they are working towards some goals, you prayed for their goals, and God will help them to achieve these goals.

Proverbs 23:18 says, *"surely there is an end; and thine expectation shall not be cut off."*

Your children can stick their vision boards on the walls of their room where they can see it every day.

Teach your children to review their goals every quarter to see how they have done and what they need to change or add to their goals. Remember goals are not cast on stones. Also, teach them to commit their goals to God individually. If they can see it with the eyes of the Spirit, they can possess it.

Habakkuk 2:2–3 say; "Write the vision, and make it plain upon tables, that he may run that readeth it. For the vision is yet for an appointed time, but at the end it shall speak, and not lie: though it tarry, wait for it; because it will surely come, it will not tarry."

83. Preparing the minds of your children will help them to have half full mentality instead of half empty mentality. They will see opportunity in every situation. This will help you and your children to focus on the positive side of life, appreciating what you have and following your goals and visions to make it better. The half empty

110 Nuggets For Excellent Parenting

mentality triggers complaints and murmuring, looking at areas where you have failed.

Proverbs 23:7 says *"For as he thinketh in his heart, so is he: Eat and drink, saith he to thee; but his heart is not with thee."*

Luke 6:45 *says "A good man out of the good treasure of his heart bringeth forth that which is good; and an evil man out of the evil treasure of his heart bringeth forth that which is evil: for of the abundance of the heart his mouth speaketh."*

Proverbs 4:23 "Keep thy heart with all diligence; for out of it are the issues of life."

SELF ESTEEM:

I have decided to look at this specifically because it is huge in the life of every human being. Whether you are a single, separated, divorced, or co-parenting or have a family where both parents live together, it is your whole responsibility to ensure you are raising children whose self-esteem is increasing as they grow. You want to raise children who can stand up for themselves, have swagger and be able to ask for their needs in today's society. Self-esteem is the value we place on ourselves and our sense of self-worth. Self-esteem can start to show from an early age, and how you relate with your children can either have positive or negative impacts on your children's self-esteem.

110 Nuggets For Excellent Parenting

What steps can you take as a parent to support your children to develop high self-esteem? The following suggestions may help you in achieving this.

84. Ensure you give your children tasks that are easy for a start and build up the level of difficulty as they progress. This will remove the feelings of failure from the children. As this goes on, identify progress in every milestone and elements of success in everything they do.

Recognize and acknowledge even the smallest success you see. If you don't see any success in a task, even stepping out to try that task is a success, encourage them and let them know you trust in them that they can try again and do it.

Mathew 18:10 says, *"Take heed that ye despise not one of these little ones"*

85. When you give your children chores, say 'thank you' to them for doing their chores. If they do not do it well, identify areas they have done well and

show them how to do it well next time. Please do not nag about it, because if you do, they will not hear the correction, they will only hear your nagging.

86. Do not underestimate what a hug can do. Hug your children and do not hold back. Touch, touch, and touch their heads! Hold their hands, and make eye contacts. Talk with them, not at them. This will make them feel great about who they are, feel accepted and will have positive impact on their self esteem.

87. Have a family meeting once a quarter; allow everyone to talk about what they see that you are doing well as a family and what they will like to see change. This will be a feedback session for everyone in the family. Most times the greatest voice we need to self-reflect may come from our children. This is an opportunity for your children to have a voice.

110 Nuggets For Excellent Parenting

88. As your children grow, their eating habits will change, they may begin to eat more and the boys may begin to eat at odd hours, getting up right in the middle of the nights to have snacks or cereal etc. There are hormonal changes and this phase will pass. I know most boys get out of bed to find something to eat. Do not call them names to label this as a negative behavior because this can damage their self-esteem.

Our son as a teenager always got out of bed to look for snacks, cereal, and fruit etc. Initially I was wondering why? But trust me, now, once he takes his dinner that is it. It is a phase and stops after a few years.

89. Your children will get to that phase where they want to wear whatever they like, no matter what you say. You may not like this, trust me, this phase will pass too. Having three girls and a boy was a kind of a handful for me.

110 Nuggets For Excellent Parenting

There was this stage that one of my girls will always buy clothes that are expensive and very tight, to the point that she has to be pulling them down each time she walks. She ends up wearing these dresses once or twice, and will always ask "Am I looking fine?" always feeling that people are looking at her. As she moved from late teenage years into adulthood, she said to me one day "mom I need to get some corporate clothes that can make me look very responsible, even as I attend job interviews." In my mind, I said thank God! At least the new corporate clothes can be worn a few times more before being discarded; maturity has come!

90. Get your children to identify things they like about themselves. Sometimes children struggle to remember things they like especially when it concerns them. Even as adults, we most times find it easier to focus on our negatives. Help them to identify their positives by letting them know things you like about them; for example, 'you are

a good helper,' 'I like your smile,' 'you are hard working,' 'you care a lot' etc. Also support them to identify the things they are good at doing and get them to practice praising themselves for the things they are able to accomplish.

91. Have an affirmation or Godly phrases or positive statements box where they can each pick out an affirmation or a positive statement every morning as you finish praying with them and they are leaving home for school. See *appendix 1* for samples of affirmations for children; you and your children can also add to this list. Affirmations will help you and your children think and speak positively about yourselves. There is power in the words that we speak. The Bible says they are Life and they are Spirits.

John 6:63 says,

"It is the spirit that quickeneth; the flesh profiteth nothing: the words that I speak unto you, they are spirit, and they are life."

FATHERS:

Dads

Dad's as strong as an ox

Dad's as tough as steel

Dad's as brave as a lion

Dad's as helpful as Google

Dad's as smart as a computer

Dad's as sneaky as a leprechaun

Dad's as jolly as Santa

Dad's as fast as sound

Dad's as funny as a comedy show

Dad's as supportive as a loyal dog

(Nwoke, O. 2014)

110 Nuggets For Excellent Parenting

From this poem, there are so many expectations on a father in every area of life starting from the family. He is expected to be strong even when he is feeling weak or struggling, and he is not expected to fear. He is expected to be very helpful even when no one thought him how to help. He is expected to be an embodiment of knowledge, joyous even when he can't pay his family's rent, be a source of laughter for his family even when he has just been fired from his job, be always ready and fast to offer support from helping with homework to rocking his child to sleep. Your children expect a 'super dad'.

I am sure that taking steps one day at a time to meet your children's expectations even halfway will be a stabilizing factor in your children's lives. It can be very hard, especially, if no one taught you how to be a father. I know there is an anointing and Grace to fulfill this God-given role.

92. The role of a father in a child's life is the first contact a child is making with a male in his or her

life. Your children expect you to be physically and emotionally available. Your behavior is expected to be a role model. Showing positive behavior and treating the mother of your children right with care and respect will be a great example to your sons and daughters.

Girls most times appear to date and marry men who are like their fathers. If your children have positive experiences with you growing up, it will positively impact their lives in the area of choices they make, ability to make the right decisions, relationships with men, self-esteem and their sense of self-worth and self-acceptance.

Ephesians 6:4 says,
"and ye fathers, provoke not your children to wrath:
but bring them up in the nurture and admonition of
the Lord."

93. Fathers are expected to leave an inheritance for their children. What are you going to be leaving for your children? Is it a good name, core values, good behavior that you taught them or what? This is the time to make the decision of what you want them to remember about you after you are gone.

They expect you to teach them as a father, do things together with them as father and son, father and daughter, take them to do their hair, play with them, give them a shower, teach your son how to be a man and your daughter, how to relate with men. You do not want to put your children in a type of situation where they are disconnected from you. You are the compass your children need to find their paths in life. You are the first man your daughters see and know, and you are the role model for your sons. According to Kachi Nwoke (2014), in his compilation of poems, "Your relationship with your sons as a father will make them to decide if they want to be like you, make a

110 Nuggets For Excellent Parenting

vow to be different from you or decide to outdo the achievements of their fathers."

94. It is an enormous responsibility to be a father. The expectations are too much and I will recommend you reflect on your strengths and weaknesses, and look for resources to support you in this role.

   A mentor will be a great idea, as well as attending some training to learn how to be an effective dad. We are all products of our environments, letting go of the past, and finding ways of supporting yourself for the present and future will be helpful to you in this role.

95. Your children are also watching the way you relate with your wife, who is their mother or step mother; treating her with kindness and love will increase the bonding you have with your children. No child wants to watch her mother being abused in any way. It is very traumatic for children to experience or watch abuse happen in the family they grow up in.

Sometimes as well, in some relationships, men experience abuse from their wives; this equally damages the child and the person being abused. Whichever way you find yourself, get help and work on yourself; get the skills you need to function as a great dad. Fatherhood is a divine role! Always go back to God and ask for wisdom to lead your family and raise your children. I believe you can achieve this if you step up and get the support you need.

SPIRITUAL:

Parenting is a physical and emotional responsibility with a spiritual compass. No one can do it alone without God's help and support from friends and family. The spiritual self of human is one of the main aspects of our being, it needs to be fed and nourished as your children grow. Neglecting the spiritual self of your children will constitute a directionless, cloudy journey in life filled with illusions and mirage.

96. Parents are commanded by God to teach and train their children. According to Deuteronomy 6 verses 6–9, *"Thou shalt teach them diligently unto*

thy children." Teach your children to embrace God and they do not have to go through life alone.

This way they are able to develop a spiritual relationship with God, understanding that with one hand in God and the other hand in their parents' they can go through life successfully without fear. It is your responsibility to raise your children well, and it is not only the responsibility of the Child Worker, Teacher, the Pastor, the Sunday school Teacher, or your own parents. God boasted with Abraham in Genesis 18 verse 19, *"For I know him; that he will command his children and his household after him, and they shall keep the way of the Lord."*

97. Pray for your children, pray over your children and pray with your children. Speak over their lives using God's Word. As a parent you have spiritual authority over your children. I *appendix II*, after the thanksgiving prayers, 150 prophetic prayers are listed in *appendix II B* for you to declare over

the lives of your children. I call them prophetic utterances using God's Word and I continue to declare them over my children.

There are also positive statements listed for you and your children. Most people refer to these positive statements or as affirmations. They are stated in the present and as you declare them over your children's lives, the Spirit of God will perfect them. See *appendix 1* for examples of these positive statements you can get your children to speak daily over their own lives.

Right from when I was pregnant, I would always put my hands on my stomach and declare prophetic prayers into my children's lives. Even after they were born, I always continued to lay my hands on them saying the same prayers.

I spoke into their future, and recently our son said "mom I heard you one night when I was little, you laid your hands on me praying for me, I shut my eyes pretending to be asleep." That memory has lived with him till date. It was tiring for me to sleep a bit, wake up and pray individually for our children; looking back today, it was worth it! Silencing and rebuking every negative spirit you see in your children works miraculously. The battle is spiritual and it is more on your knees than in your mouth!

98. Teach them to pray for themselves and tap into the Grace of God. This way, they are able to understand the love of God for them and not lack a sense of self-worth. They will also understand the Grace of God to forgive themselves and others.

Hebrews 13:6 says:

"So we may boldly say, The Lord is my Helper, and I will not fear what man shall do unto me."

99. What are the issues or patterns in your own family and your spouse's family? Are there issues like abuse, separation, divorce, illnesses such as diabetes, heart disease, cancer, untimely deaths, lack

110 Nuggets For Excellent Parenting

of focus, addictions, incestuous relationships, late marriages etc.? Start now to pray against these negative patterns and rebuke the spirits behind them using God's Words.

There is also the need to teach your children the right values that will help them to stop repeating these negative patterns and break the cycle. See Genesis 20:2; Abraham lied about Sarah saying *"she is my sister"* and not his wife. His son Isaac did the same thing in Genesis 26:7, saying about Rebekah, *"she is my sister"* and not his wife. What is that evil that has passed through your own generation? It is time to stop the spread. Stop the cycle using the Word of God, prayers, changing your behaviors, stop playing the victim and taking accountability for your actions.

100. Teach them to honor and respect you as their parent. Exodus *20:12 says, "Honor thy father and thy mother: that thy days may be long upon the land which the LORD thy God giveth thee."*

This is a command from God with a promise of long life attached to it. Ephesians 6:4 also states that, *"And, ye fathers, provoke not your children to wrath: but bring them up in the nurture and admonition of the Lord."*

Building relationship with your children is very important, and giving them opportunity to be real with you even when it makes you uncomfortable is very important. In our family meeting one morning, one of my children said to me, "Mom, you don't listen to me." That broke my heart because I thought I really did listen to my children's needs. I reflected on it and realized it was true. I took accountability, and apologized to her. I am still working on myself and making progress.

ALL PARENTS: CARING FOR YOURSELF AS A PARENT

Caring for yourself as a parent is a very important aspect of your role as you raise your children. If you do not care for yourself, it is like driving a car for so long without taking it to a workshop for maintenance. I am not an auto mechanic, but I know that servicing a car involves oil change, wheel alignments, checking the brakes and general maintenance.

Most times, as parents we drive ourselves to a halt before we take some time to rest, take a-me-time, or ask for respite or support. You need to take care of

110 Nuggets For Excellent Parenting

your physical, emotional and spiritual wellbeing; this will help you to be an effective parent.

101. What is it that causes you a lot of stress? It is your responsibility to identify your own sources of stress. Is there a particular thing that makes you worry all the time? Is it your finances? Are you playing the role of both parents in your children's lives? Is there a conversation that needs to happen, what is the elephant in the room? Is your relationship with your spouse stressful? Get professional help and ask for your needs in an assertive manner. Your life is important. Take care of these stresses, so you can function effectively and live longer, your health is important! Effective parenting requires effective health.

102. As a parent, there is need for you to have and develop a strong supportive network that you can connect with, where you can continuously draw strength for the task of parenting. If you have

110 Nuggets For Excellent Parenting

support networks such as church, home groups, circle of supportive friends or supportive family; this will be a huge source of strength. Make sure you are active in any of these support circles that you belong to. Through this you will have the opportunity to be encouraged by your supports and you can learn from others too. I go to church and have some close friends in my home church that I connect with for supports.

103. Self-care is very important for you as a parent. On a daily basis, what do you do to recharge yourself? Even something as small as having a warm shower at the end of the day, taking a walk, watching your favorite program, using the gym, having a nap etc. The list is inexhaustible!

Find out what you can do every day for YOU and this will help you relax, recharge and regain your strength to continue the journey of parenting because it is a life journey. I go for walks, have long shower, pray, watch my favorite TV programs etc. These help me to relax and not take life too seriously!

104. Practice taking sometime to yourself to do what you love and let that be a 'me time' for you. At least one Saturday in a month, get someone to look after your children and you can take some time to yourself. Actually leave home if your children are at home with another adult or take them to your parents or a supportive family or neighbor and get some rest, a long sleep, or go for coffee with friends, go to the mall, do your nails or something you love and you know it will make you feel great.

What was your hobby before the life job of parenting started? It's time to pick it up again. Find time no matter how small. Most times as parents, we get so dependent on our children emotionally that we have virtually stopped identifying what we feel or need, forgetting that our children will grow and they will live their lives totally separately from us. It is not when they are grown, and we start feeling lonely that we will begin to plan our own lives. Start now parents!

105. Believe in your competence to parent your children. Parenting is actually a skill you learn while on the job as I said earlier. If you feel inadequate, ask for help, take a course, talk to a professional and pray for wisdom and pray for your children too. There are lots of trainings you can do and these trainings can be very insightful.

Accept your mistakes as opportunities for learning. Note that you are NOT your mistakes. Also, if your parents showed you an example of how not to be a parent, it is time for you to do a parenting course. It is short and there may be some free courses around you. You can also have a mentor who can support you all the way through at every stage, because every stage is a fresh challenge. Remember, there is no perfect parent; you are striving towards excellence and not perfection.

106. Look after your body, soul and spirit. For your body, eat well, sleep well, and nap in-between as your children nap during the day; this time should not be the time for laundry, cleaning etc. Raise up your feet and rest with your children. Do not drink, smoke, or do drugs. See your physician at least three times a year for full physical checkups. Get adequate quantity of your natural produce of fruits and vegetables.

For your soul, be mindful of negative emotions and what you allow into your soul. For your spirit, pray, meditate and read your Bible daily, have a quiet time where you can draw strength for the day because you are a spirit being. Mostly, live a life of forgiveness. Sometimes it can be hard but it is a healthy choice to make for yourself; it is not for the person who has offended you.

110 Nuggets For Excellent Parenting

107. Treat yourself kindly the way you will treat a friend you love. Have self-compassion for yourself. Dr. Catherine Keith (2013), in her work on self-esteem, says that self-compassion is "our ability to treat ourselves with the same kindness and care we would treat a friend we love."

Give gifts to yourself regularly because you are working hard, parenting is hard work and when we are working parents, the job is tripled because as you close from work, the greater job begins at home. Buy yourself flowers from time to time and any other thing you love that can help to make you feel good. I buy gifts for myself from time to time as a pat on my back that I am doing a great job in my parenting role. You are doing a great job in taking time to raise your children. Please acknowledge this for yourself.

108. Put some efforts into improving your personal appearance as this will go a long way in making you feel good about yourself. Wear colors you

love if you are a mother and if you are a dad, get those colors or textures of clothes or shirts you love. As people see you and admire what you are putting on, it may help you feel a lot better about yourself. It does not have to be expensive; consignment stores are handy, items on sale e.tc.

Understand that raising children is a great work that will slow down your career, education, and other major areas of your lives; especially for mothers. However, it is a commitment that gives rewards that money cannot buy; it is a daily investment that you do not have opportunity to go back to yesterday. Therefore, it is necessary to do all you can to make every moment count in your life and in the lives of your children.

Begin to see every day as a gift from God, embrace it with joy and laughter because it is a PRESENT! Focusing on the past and worrying about the future messes up your present because your two legs are spread between your past and future, so there is no foot to step on the present. This means as parents there is a great need for you to make a conscious effort to enjoy the present moment as you raise your children.

109. Finally, there is need to understand that the support of your community is highly invaluable in raising your children. Your extended family, your church, the school, teachers and professionals, the government agencies, everyone has one goal for you and your children. That great goal is to support you in raising children who will become good citizens of the society we live in and fulfill their destinies. Use these supports to make this tough job which is an invaluable gift, lighter, enjoyable, fun and successful. You may be raising the next President, CEO, and or College Principal; above all you are definitely raising the next fathers and mothers.

Breaking the negative patterns you experienced and continuing or starting the cycle of positive patterns in your generation is a great choice you can make today, so step out and be that great parent God has purposed for you. The power of God lives within you! All great things are possible if you believe and take actions!

110. According to John .F.Kennedy (1963), the late President of United States, "we can say with some assurance that, although children may be victims of fate, they will not be the victims of our neglect." Children are placed in your custody, and you will give account of the role you played daily in raising them. You have a great person in your hands that the world will depend on for tomorrow, and you are a great tool in supporting them to fulfill their destinies.

Are there are times you have done all you can, and you still beat yourself down, feeling you have not done enough? Maybe a particular child is not behaving appropriately? Get the supports that you need. Parenting is a tough but rewarding job. Understand that before you became parents, you were first a boy and a girl. There may still be some "little boy or little girl" issues that you need to work on. Working on yourself is a life journey; continue to do so as you parent your children. Good luck in your wonderful and rewarding parenting role! The Grace of God is sufficient for you.

REFERENCES

1. Black, C. (2001). *It will never happen to me: Growing up with addiction as youngsters, adolescents, adults* (2nd ed., Rev.). Bainbridge Island, WA: MAC Publishing.
2. Black, C. (2010). Understanding the pain of abandonment: Living with repeated abandonment experiences creates toxic shame. In The Many Faces of Addiction. Retrieved from https://www.psychologytoday.com/blog/the-many-faces-addiction/201006/understanding-the-pain-abandonment

3. Coloroso, B. (2010). Kids are worth it! Raising resilient, responsible, compassionate kids. Toronto, Ontario: Penguin Canada.
4. Covington S. (2008). A woman's journal, helping women recover: A program for treating addictions. San Francisco, CA: Jossey-Bass Publishing.
5. Hermes, S. (2009). The art of assertiveness: Practical skills for positive communication [DVD]. Minneapolis: Hazelden Publishing.
6. Keith, D. (2013). How's your self-esteem? Unpublished manuscript.
7. Kennedy, J.F. (1963). Remarks upon signing the maternal and child health mental retardation planning bill (434). Retrieved from http://www.jfklibrary.org/Asset-Viewer/Archives/JFKPOF-047–038.aspx
8. Kennedy, J. F. (1963). Presidential Library and Museum: John F. Kennedy Quotations. Retrieved from http://www.jfklibrary.org/Research/Research-Aids/Ready-Reference/JFK-Quotations.aspx

9. *Larsen, E. (1991).* Dealing with Discouragement [DVD]. Minneapolis *10.*

10. *Nwoke, O. (2014).* Kachi's collections: A compilation of poems. *Unpublished manuscript.*

11. The Holy Bible, King James Version. Thomas Nelson Inc.: 1972. Nashville.

APPENDIX 1:

POWERFUL GODLY AFFIRMATIONS FOR YOU AND YOUR CHILDREN

These are positive statements you and your children can personally repeat daily and it's a great support for building their future. Get your children to say them loud.

1. I am fearfully and wonderfully made by God.
2. I am kind.
3. I am creative.
4. I am beautiful inside and outside.
5. I am a handsome boy.
6. I am a beautiful girl.
7. I love myself.

110 Nuggets For Excellent Parenting

8. I am full of wisdom.

9. I am very helpful.

10. I am happy.

11. I am joyful.

12. I am special to God.

13. I am a good child.

14. I am funny and playful.

15. I have a great sense of humor.

16. I am lovable.

17. I am alive and well.

18. Today, I am kind to myself.

19. I am unique and special.

20. I am not my mistakes.

21. I am a child of God.

22. I am a good friend.

23. Today, I am responsible for my actions.

24. Today, I have the right to say NO to wrong suggestions.

25. Today, I will listen to my parents and God.

26. Today, I will ask questions if I don't understand.

27. Today, I am a good student.

110 Nuggets For Excellent Parenting

28. Today, I am teachable.

29. Today, I will learn good things from my parents and teachers.

30. Today, I am not afraid.

31. Today, I have Faith in God.

32. Today, I feel good about myself.

33. Today, I love my body.

34. I am caring.

35. Today, I accept the love of God into my life.

36. Today, I will ask for my needs.

37. Today, I am assertive in my communication.

38. I am very happy I was born by my parents.

39. I am a healthy person.

40. Today, I will relax and have fun.

41. Today, the joy of the Lord is my strength.

42. Today, I am blessed by God.

43. Today, I am anointed by God.

44. Today, I am covered in the blood of Jesus Christ.

45. Today, God is working through me and for me.

46. My life counts in God's plans.

47. Today, I have the right to my feelings.

110 Nuggets For Excellent Parenting

48. Today, my feet are dipped in oil of extraordinary favor.

49. Today, no weapon fashioned against me shall prosper.

50. Today, I will enjoy my play with my siblings and friends.

51. Today, I will meditate on the Word of God.

52. Today, I will treat myself with love and kindness.

53. Today, I will speak the truth in all things.

54. Today, I have unspeakable joy.

55. Today, I will listen and learn new things.

56. God is doing awesome things for me.

57. Today, I am walking according to God's purpose for my life.

58. Today, I will hug my friends and family and receive hugs too.

59. Today, I will eat well including my fruits and vegetables.

60. Today, I will say my prayers and believe that God has answered them.

110 Nuggets For Excellent Parenting

61. Today, when people say I am beautiful, I will smile and say thank you.

62. Today, I will encourage a friend.

63. Today, I will do a good thing for someone without getting caught.

64. Today, I like my hair.

65. Today, I love my smiles.

66. Today, I will not worry about tomorrow.

67. Today, I know I am learning and growing as I should.

68. Today, I see great success in my life.

69. Today, I am a great helper.

70. Today, I will clean up my mess after me.

71. Today, I will laugh aloud.

72. Today, I will respect everyone around me.

73. Today, I will dance and enjoy my play with my friends.

74. My life is filled with purpose and meaning.

75. Today, I will take good care of myself.

76. Today, I will ask for help when I need it.

77. I feel happy with the things I do.

110 Nuggets For Excellent Parenting

78. I give love to myself.

79. Today, the angels of God are watching over me.

80. Today, I have excellence in every area of my life.

81. Today, I will make the right choices.

82. Today, I have room for growth.

83. Today, I will listen and learn from feedback from my parents, teachers and supportive friends.

84. Today, I see a great future for me.

85. Today, I will speak positively about myself and others.

86. Today, I am forgiving of myself and others.

87. Today, I will acknowledge my fears, talk about them and put them in God's hands.

88. Today, I will sing and dance.

89. Today, I am gentle with myself.

90. Today, I will take responsibility for my actions.

91. Today, I will make time for myself.

92. Today, I will say "I love you" to people I love.

93. Today, I realize that mistakes are opportunities for learning.

94. Today, I hope for the best.

110 Nuggets For Excellent Parenting

95. Today, I am considerate of others.

96. Today, I will have fun, be a child that I am and have fun.

97. Today, I will live one day at a time.

98. Today, I will embrace life with joy and strength from God.

99. I know down deeply in my heart that I am a child of God.

100. I am a carrier of the Glory of God.

101. Today, I have faith in God.

102. Today, I know who I am in Christ Jesus.

103. Today, God is helping me.

104. Today, Jesus Christ has connected me to the Father and Eternity.

105. Today, I have Eternal Life.

106. Today, I will be honest about my feelings and everything that are around me.

107. Today, I am a child of Integrity.

108. Today, God is doing a new thing in my Life.

109. Today, my feet are dipped in the oil of greatness.

110. Today, I will not beg for bread.

110 Nuggets For Excellent Parenting

111. Today, I am not afraid because God is fighting for me and I will continue to hold my peace.

112. Today, the Word of God will work for me.

113. Today, every red sea before me is parted already in Jesus Mighty Name.

114. Today, I am shinning above my peers because I am anointed of God.

115. Today, I have more understanding than my teachers.

116. Today, my heart is illuminated by the Word and Glory of God.

117. Today, I am above and not beneath in Jesus Name.

118. Today, the Holy Ghost is embracing me.

119. Today, God has visited me with His Divine Presence.

120. Today, God will perfect All that concern me.

APPENDIX II :

THANKSGIVING PRAYERS AND PROPHETIC PRAYERS FOR YOU AND YOUR CHILDREN

Call your child's name and declare using these personalized prophetic prayer points in Jesus Name, with Biblical References
(King James Version)

A. **PRAYER OF THANKSGIVING: (PSALM 100:1-END)**

1. Thank you Lord for blessing me with these wonderful children.
2. Thank you Lord for their safe delivery and protection from time of conception to today.
3. Lord I bless you for the privilege to be a parent.

110 Nuggets For Excellent Parenting

4. Thank you Jesus for the Joy that comes from being a parent.

5. Thank you Father for the Grace to nurture and raise these children for you.

6. Thank you Lord for helping me and giving me wisdom to be a great father/ great mother to my children.

7. Thank you Lord for giving me provisions to meet all the responsibilities that comes from being a parent.

8. Thank you Lord for the days I don't know what to say or do as a parent, and you put the right words in my mouth at that moment of need.

9. Thank you Lord for the times I say the right things and take the right actions and my children may perceive them as wrong; but at the end you make all things right for your Glory.

10. Thank you Lord for those days I don't feel like being a parent, and you step in and multiply your Grace upon me afresh.

APPENDIX II B:
PROPHETIC PRAYERS FOR YOU AND YOUR CHILDREN

Prophetic prayers will help you speak into the future of your children and strategically position them for greatness to fulfill their destinies. Mention the names of your children and declare these prayers.

1. Isaiah 65:23: You will not labor in vain, and you will NOT bring forth for trouble.
2. Isaiah 44:3: The Lord has poured out His Spirit on you and His blessings on you all the days of your life.
3. Psalm 91:10: No evil will befall you anywhere you go.

4. Psalm 91:11–12: For God will order His angels to protect you wherever you go. They are holding you up with their hands so you won't dash your foot on a stone

5. Psalm 91:16: The Lord will continuously satisfy you with long life and show you His salvation.

6. Psalm 112:2: You my children will be successful everywhere you go and in all you do; and your entire generation will be blessed because I am the righteousness of God.

7. Jeremiah 32:39: The Lord has given you one heart and one purpose: to worship Him forever, for your own good and for the good of all your descendants.

8. Acts 2:39: This promise of God is for you and they will work for you because you have been called by the Lord our God.

9. Luke 2:46–47: All will be astonished at your level of wisdom and answers.

10. Psalm 16:7: The Lord is giving you Counsel always and you will always receive His instructions in the night seasons.

110 Nuggets For Excellent Parenting

11. Jeremiah 29:11: The thoughts of God towards you are that of good all the days of your life.

12. Isaiah 8:9–10: The Lord has broken in pieces all those who have conspired together to do you evil.

13. Psalm 18:28–29: The Lord will always lighten up your path and God has filled you with power to leap over any kind of wall.

14. Psalm 18:29: In God's strength you have crushed an army; with God's strength you have scaled any wall.

15. Psalm 92:10: God has made you as strong as a wild ox. God has anointed you with the fresh oil. You have risen higher than your peers in every area of your life.

16. Luke 2:52: You will continuously increase in wisdom and stature and in favor with God and man.

17. 3 John:2: God is prospering your soul daily and everything about you is prosperous.

18. Luke 1:32: You are Great and you will come out Great in everything that concerns you.

110 Nuggets For Excellent Parenting

19. Exodus 23:25–26: You are serving the Lord and God has blessed your bread and your water and *NO disease* will come near you all the days of your life.

20. Psalm 115:14: The Lord will continue to increase you more and more in every area of your life all the days of your life.

21. Exodus 14:14: The Lord will continuously fight for you and you will hold your peace.

22. Isaiah 65:20: You will live very long and you will fulfill your days and destiny.

23. Revelations 12:11: You have overcome by the blood of the lamb and by the word of your testimony.

24. Galatians 3:29: You are Christ's and His heirs according to the Promise, your inheritance is in Christ Jesus.

25. Psalm 71:7: You are a wonder unto many and God is your strong refuge.

110 Nuggets For Excellent Parenting

26. Deuteronomy 15:6: The Lord has blessed you as He has promised, you shall lend unto many nations and you shall not borrow.

27. Deuteronomy 28:6: You are blessed in going out and you are blessed in coming in.

28. Deuteronomy 28:1: You are diligently serving the Lord and God has set you above all the nations of the earth.

29. Deuteronomy 28:11: God has caused your enemies to be smitten before your faces.

30. I Samuel 2:26: As you grow, you are growing in favor with God and everyone you meet in life.

31. I Samuel 3:19: The Lord will always be with you and none of His Words concerning your life will ever fall to the ground.

32. I Samuel 3:10: You will hear God expressly and you will obey His Word.

33. Genesis 6:8: You will find Grace in the eyes of the Lord and His Grace and Word will lighten your path all the days of your life.

110 Nuggets For Excellent Parenting

34. Genesis 8:1: God will always remember you for good.

35. Genesis 12:2: The Lord will bless you and make your name Great anywhere you go and in anything you lay your hands on to do.

36. Genesis 12:3: God Almighty will bless them that bless thee and curse them that curse thee.

37. Genesis 15:1: Almighty God is your shield and exceeding great reward.

38. Genesis 17:1: You will walk before God all the days of your life and God will perfect everything that concerns you.

39. Genesis 17:5: The Lord has changed your name to reflect His Glory.

40. Genesis 18:17: God will always reveal His Plans to you all the days of your life.

41. Genesis 24:60: The Lord will empower you to always possess the gates of your enemies.

42. Genesis 26:22: The Lord will make room for you anywhere you go.

110 Nuggets For Excellent Parenting

43. Genesis 39:21: The Lord will be with you and He will show you mercy and favor in the sight of anyone you meet.

44. Exodus 13:21–22: The Almighty God will lead you by the pillar of cloud of His Presence and by the Pillar of Fire of His Presence all the days of your life.

45. Exodus 14:13 -15: You are going forward because the Almighty God is fighting for you and you are surrounded with the Peace of the Lord because He is your Jehovah Shalom.

46. Exodus 14:31, 15:3: You will see the great work the Lord will continue to do upon your enemies and they will fear the Jehovah Gibeoah (the man of war) that you serve.

47. Exodus 23:20: The Lord shall always send His angels to keep you and bring you into the place He has prepared for you.

48. Exodus 33:18: The Lord will continuously show you His Glory.

110 Nuggets For Excellent Parenting

49. Psalm 5:12: The Lord will bless you and compass you with favor as a shield all the days of your life.

50. Psalm 7:9: The wickedness of the wicked has come to an end in every area of your life.

51. Psalm 16:6: The lines are fallen unto you in pleasant places and I know that in the name of Jesus Christ you have a goodly heritage.

52. Psalm 29:11: The Lord will give you strength always and the Lord will bless you with His peace.

53. Psalm 31:15: Your times are in the hand of the Lord, the Lord has delivered you from your enemies and from them that persecute you.

54. Psalm 33:18: Behold; the eyes of the Lord will continue to be upon you because you fear Him and because you hope in His Mercy.

55. Psalm 37:25: Because you are the righteousness of God, you will never beg for bread.

56. Psalm 40:8: You will always take delight in doing God's Will and God's Words are written in your heart all the days of your life.

110 Nuggets For Excellent Parenting

57. Psalm 48:14: For this God is your God forever and ever, He will be your Guide even unto the end.

58. Psalm 68:1–2: Let God arise for you and let your enemies be scattered and let them that hate you flee before your God and as smoke is driven away let God drive your enemies away.

59. Psalm 71:21: The Lord shall increase your greatness and comfort you on every side.

60. Psalm 75:6–7: God will promote you above your peers on every side all the days of your life.

61. Psalm 75:10: The Lord will exalt your horn always and The Lord will cut off the horns of your enemies.

62. Psalm 78:72: The Lord will feed you always according to the integrity of His heart and He will guide you all the days of your life by the skillfulness of His Hands.

63. Psalm 84:11: The Lord is your sun and shield; He has given you Grace and Glory, NO Good thing will he withhold from you as you walk uprightly with Him.

110 Nuggets For Excellent Parenting

64. Psalm 86:11: The Lord will continuously teach you His ways and you will walk in God's truth and the Lord will unite your heart to fear Him all the days of your life.

65. Psalm 89:1: You will sing of the mercies of the Lord forever and with your mouth will you make known God's faithfulness to all Generations.

66. Psalm 89:34–35: The Lord will NOT break His covenant to you and will not alter His promises concerning your life. The Lord has sworn by His Holiness that He will not lie to you.

67. Psalm 102:13: The Lord shall arise and have mercy upon you, for the time to favor you has come, yes the set time is now.

68. Psalm 103:17: The mercies of the Lord upon your life is from everlasting to everlasting and His righteousness is upon you all the days of your life.

69. Psalm 115:14: The Lord shall increase you more and more on every side, including all your generations.

70. Psalm 119:105: The Word of God is a lamp unto your feet and a light unto your path all the days of your life.

71. Psalm 119:99–100: You have more understanding than all your teachers because you keep the precepts of God.

72. Psalm 125:1: Because you trust the Lord, your life is like mount Zion which cannot be moved but abideth forever.

73. Psalm 125:3: The rod of the wicked will not rest upon you all the days of your life.

74. Psalm 138:8: The Lord will perfect that which concerns you all the days of your life.

75. Psalm 144:12: You my sons, you are as plants grown up in your youth and you my daughters, are as corner stones, polished after the similitude of a palace.

76. Psalm 147:11: The Lord is taking pleasure in you because you fear Him and because you hope in His Mercies all the days of your life.

110 Nuggets For Excellent Parenting

77. Psalm 150: I praise God for your life and your life is a great praise unto God all the days of your life.

78. Proverbs 10:22: You are blessings from the Lord and you will not add any sorrow to me.

79. Proverbs 13:20: You will walk with the wise all the days of your life. You will never walk with fools.

80. Proverbs 18:16: Your gift will make room for you and bring you before kings.

81. Isaiah 1:19: You are willing and obedient to God and you shall eat the good of the land.

82. Isaiah 6:8: You will answer to the call of the Lord all the days of your life.

83. Isaiah 8:9–10: Every counsel of the enemy over your life is broken in pieces and it shall not stand for God is with you.

84. Isaiah 8:18: You are for signs and wonders all over the earth and all the days of your life.

85. Isaiah 11:2: The Spirit of the Lord God is resting upon you, spirit of wisdom and understanding, spirit of counsel and might, spirit of knowledge and of the fear of the Lord.

86. Isaiah 30:21: You will hear the voice of the Lord behind you directing and leading you anywhere you go.

87. Isaiah 33:6: Wisdom and knowledge shall be the stability of your life and strength of salvation and you will treasure from fearing the Lord.

88. Isaiah 45:2–3: The Lord has gone ahead of you and made your ways straight and God has broken every barrier in your life.

89. Isaiah 49:15–15: The Lord will never forget you, because He has graven you in the palms of His hands.

90. Isaiah 49:24–26: The Lord will contend with them that contend with you, the Lord will save you and continuously feed your enemies with their own blood.

91. Isaiah 50:7: The Lord God will help you, and you shall not be disgraced, you will not be put to shame.

92. Isaiah 54:13: You are taught by the Lord and great shall be your peace all the days of your life.

110 Nuggets For Excellent Parenting

93. Isaiah 54:17: No weapon fashioned against you shall prosper and every tongue that rises against you in judgment, I condemn.

94. Isaiah 60:1: Arise and shine, for the Glory of God is risen upon you.

95. Jeremiah 1:5: The Lord has ordained you and set you apart for greatness in your generation.

96. Jeremiah 32:17& 27: The Lord will meet all your needs because there is nothing too difficult for him to do.

97. Jeremiah 33:3: Each time you call on God, He will answer you and show you great and mighty things.

98. Daniel 6:3: You are preferred above your peers because you have an excellent Spirit in you.

99. Daniel 11:32: Because you know your God, you shall be strong and you shall do exploits.

100. Joel 2:28: The Lord has poured out His Spirit upon you. You will prophecy and see heavenly visions.

101. John 3:16: You will know the Lord all the days of your life and you will not miss heaven.

102. James 1:17: You are a good and perfect gift because you came from the Lord.

103. Peter 5:6: The Lord will exalt you as you humble yourself underneath His mighty arm and you will always cast your cares upon Him because He cares for you.

104. Galatians 5:22–23: You are filled with the character of God and you will manifest the fruits of the Spirit—love, joy, peace, patience, kindness, goodness, faithfulness, gentleness, and self-control.

105. Ephesians 6:10: You are strong in the Lord and in the power of His might and you are putting on the whole armor of God all the days of your life.

106. Luke 2:52: You are growing in wisdom and stature as Jesus grew and you are having favor with God and the people.

107. Acts 2:1–4: You will have a Pentecost experience all the days of your life and Holy Spirit of God will guide you into all truth.

110 Nuggets For Excellent Parenting

108. Revelation 12:11: You will always overcome by the blood of the lamb and by the word of your testimony.

109. Revelations 19:7–8: You will always be ready for the coming of the Lord and you will not miss Heaven.

110. Proverbs 29:17: The Lord has given me wisdom to raise you according to God's principles and you will not depart from them.

111. Esther 2:17: The Lord will continuously love you and you will obtain Grace and Favor in His sight above all in your generation.

112. Job 5:12: In your life the Lord has disappointed the devices of the crafty, and their hands cannot perform their enterprise.

113. Job 5:14: Your enemies have met with darkness in the day time and they are groping in the noon day as in the night.

114. Job 5:26: The Lord has blessed you with healthy long life.

110 Nuggets For Excellent Parenting

115. Job 10:12: God has given you life and favor; He will visit you continuously and preserve your spirit.

116. Job 22:28–29: The Lord will honor your word and there shall always be a lifting up for you even when your peers are cast down.

117. Numbers 23:19: God will establish all his promises in your life.

118. Numbers 23:20 & 23: The Lord has blessed you and you are blessed beyond measure. There is NO enchantment against you and your generations.

119. Deuteronomy 5:33: You will continuously walk in the ways of the Lord, it shall be well with you and your days are prolonged.

120. Deuteronomy 7:13 & 14: The Lord will bless you and multiply you, bless the fruit of your womb and NONE shall be barren in your generation.

121. Deuteronomy 8:18: You will never forget God, You will remember Him all the days of your life because He is the one that has given you power to make wealth.

110 Nuggets For Excellent Parenting

122. Deuteronomy 29:29: The Lord will reveal all His secrets to you in every area of your life.

123. Deuteronomy 32:12: You will not serve any strange God all the days of your life.

124. Joshua 1:5: The Lord will be with you and NO man can stand before you all the days of your life.

125. I Kings 5:4: The Lord God has given you rest on every side ALL the days of your life.

126. I Kings 2:9: God has put a double portion of His Spirit upon you.

127. I Chronicles 4:10: The Lord bless you, the Lord enlarge your coast, His hands will be with you and keep you from evil.

128. II Chronicles 6:17: There will always be verifiable evidence in your life that you are a child of God and serving God.

129. II Chronicles 20:15: The Lord will fight your battles and you will NOT be afraid of your enemies.

130. Ezra 8:22: The hand of the Lord is upon you for good and His Power and wrath are against them that fight with you.

110 Nuggets For Excellent Parenting

131. Nehemiah 13:31: The Lord will remember you for good.

132. Leviticus 26:5–6: The Lord will give you rain in due season, your land will yield her increase and you will eat your bread to the full and dwell in your land safely.

133. Leviticus 26:9: The Lord will honor you, make you fruitful, multiply you and continuously establish His Covenants with you.

134. Numbers 6:24 -27: The Lord bless you, make His face to shine upon you, be gracious unto thee, lift up His Countenance upon you and give you peace.

135. Numbers 12:8: The Lord will speak with you mouth to mouth all the days of your life like He spoke to Moses.

136. Number 13:30: The Lord will give you an unusual boldness and you will possess the land of your enemies.

137. Leviticus 17:11: The blood of Jesus has made an atonement for your soul and this covering of

His Blood will continually keep you safe all the days of your life.

138. Job 36:11: As you obey and serve the Lord, you will spend your days in prosperity and your years in pleasure.

139. Mathew 2:10: You are the Star of Glory in your generation.

140. Mathew 2:13: Every Herod after your life, the Lord has destroyed.

141. Mathew 15:13: Every plant that the Lord has not planted in your life shall be rooted out.

142. Mark 10:27, Luke 1:37: Nothing shall be impossible in your life.

143. Mathew 3:16: The Heavens are open over your life.

144. John 1:12: As you have received God, you have been given the power to become the son of God.

145. John 10:5: You will hear the voice of God and will not follow a stranger.

146. Acts 2:4: You are filled with the Holy Ghost and with Power.

110 Nuggets For Excellent Parenting

147. Acts 20:32: I commend you to God and to the Word of His Grace which is able to build you up, and to give you an inheritance among all who are sanctified.

148. 2 Thessalonians 1 vs. 6. It is a righteous thing for God to bring tribulations to them that trouble you.

149. Proverbs 4:26. The Lord will establish you in Heaven and He shall make your name to be known on earth.

150. 2 Peter 3:9: The Lord is not slack concerning His Promises to you. Every Word of God over your Life shall be FULFILLED IN Jesus' Name!

CPSIA information can be obtained
at www.ICGtesting.com
Printed in the USA
LVOW04s0401290316
481153LV00009B/32/P